BURRITOS!

DONNA KELLY AND SANDRA HOOPES

Photographs by David Daniels

GIBBS SMITH
TO ENRICH AND INSPIRE HUMANKIND

This book is dedicated to passionate home cooks who fill
their lives—and their food—with flavor and zest! —D. K.

To family and friends who make "home for dinner" my favorite words. —S.H.

First Edition
19 18 17 16 15   5 4 3 2 1

Text © 2015 Donna Kelly and Sandra Hoopes
Photographs © 2015 David Daniels Photography

Published by
Gibbs Smith
P.O. Box 667
Layton, Utah 84041

1.800.835.4993 orders
www.gibbs-smith.com

Designed by Katie Jennings Design
Food styled by Donna Kelly and Sandra Hoopes

Printed and bound in Hong Kong
Gibbs Smith books are printed on paper produced
from sustainable PEFC-certified forest/controlled
wood source. Learn more at www.pefc.org.

Library of Congress Cataloging-in-Publication
Data

Kelly, Donna, 1955-
  Burritos / Donna Kelly and Sandra Hoopes. —
First Edition.
      pages cm
  Includes index.
  ISBN 978-1-4236-3946-6
  1. Burritos (Cooking) I. Hoopes, Sandra. II. Title.
  TX836.K448 2015
  641.82—dc23
                                              2015004976

CONTENTS

Burrito Basics   4

Burrito Tips and Tricks   6

Rise and Shine   11

Updated Classics   22

New South of the Border   41

All-American Classics   62

Around the Globe   86

Sweet Treats   113

Sauces   122

Index   126

BURRITO BASICS

Burritos are traditionally rolled into a bundle for easy transportable eating. Here are instructions for the traditional burrito method—plus a few new styles!

Traditional Rolled Burritos

We use the standard method for rolling burritos. Place filling along the side of the tortilla nearest to you and then roll just a bit; make one complete roll away from you and then tuck sides toward the middle and then continue rolling burrito until filling is completely surrounded by the tortilla, making a cylinder shape. Each of the recipes in this book is designed to make 4 to 6 burritos, depending on how much filling you like in each burrito, using flour tortillas that are 12 inches in diameter.

Crispy Burritos

Roll burritos according to the Traditional Rolled Burritos method above. At the end of the rolling, add a little water with your finger along the edge of the tortilla and then finish rolling and place seam side down on a flat surface. Let sit for a minute or two. Heat a large, nonstick dry skillet over medium heat. Brush burrito lightly with a little vegetable oil and place in skillet, seam side down. Cook until outside of burrito is golden brown, turning with tongs frequently as needed to brown entire outside of burrito. You can also cook on a preheated outdoor grill or grill pan for a unique presentation.

Chimichangas

Roll burritos according to the Traditional Rolled Burritos method. In a deep fryer or large skillet, heat vegetable oil to 350 degrees. Fry the burritos, turning frequently so that all sides are golden brown and crispy.

Burrito Spirals

Roll burritos according to the Traditional Rolled Burritos method. Let sit for a few minutes. Using a large serrated knife, carefully cut burritos into 2- or 3-inch-thick slices. Using a wide spatula, carefully place slices on serving plates, cut sides up.

Burrito Bowls

You can skip the tortilla and turn all of the recipes in this book into a Burrito Bowl, layering the ingredients in a bowl instead of rolled into a tortilla.

Burrito Jars

One great way to transport a burrito to be eaten later is to make a burrito jar. Layer the ingredients that need to be heated in the bottom of a glass jar. Place ingredients such as lettuce and tomato that do not need heating at the top of the jar. Wrap a tortilla separately and store at room temperature.

When ready to assemble the burrito, lay the tortilla on a flat surface and pour out the fresh ingredients that do not need to be heated. Heat the ingredients left in the bottom of the jar in a microwave oven and then spoon onto the burrito. Roll and enjoy!

Freezing Burritos

To freeze burritos for later use, start with room-temperature filling and tortillas. Roll burritos tightly and then freeze on a baking sheet. When fully frozen, wrap in aluminum foil or place in a ziplock bag and freeze. To reheat burrito, bake in foil on a baking sheet at 350 degrees for about 30 minutes.

BURRITO TIPS AND TRICKS

Quick Refried Beans

1 (15-ounce) can any beans, drained and rinsed

Water, as needed

1 teaspoon garlic powder

1 to 2 teaspoons cayenne pepper or
hot sauce of choice

2 slices bacon (for vegetarian beans replace
with 1 tablespoon butter or oil)

1 to 2 ounces cheese (cheddar, Monterey Jack,
Gouda, etc.), grated

Salt and freshly ground pepper, to taste

Turn any beans into refried beans! Soft beans such as pinto, black, white, navy, and cannellini work best.

Process the beans, garlic powder, and hot sauce in a food processor until very smooth, adding a little water, if needed, to process.

Heat a large skillet to medium-high heat. Add bacon and cook, turning frequently, until most of fat is rendered and bacon is browned. Remove bacon and reserve for another use. (If making vegetarian beans, add butter to skillet instead of bacon and melt butter.) Add puréed bean mixture. Let sit for about 2 minutes, until beans begin to lightly brown on bottom. Stir, folding browned bottom crust into the beans.

Add cheese and stir until melted. Add salt and pepper. Add in water, a little at a time, to reach desired creamy texture, similar to cooked oatmeal.

☀ Makes 1½ cups

Rotisserie Chicken

Throughout this book, cooked chicken is sometimes used as an ingredient. One good shortcut is to use purchased rotisserie chicken and then remove the meat from the chicken in large chunks, discarding skin and bones. One 2 1/2-pound chicken will result in about 4 cups cooked, shredded chicken meat.

Rice

Rice is frequently used in burrito recipes, and is more than just a filler. Rice adds texture to burritos and absorbs juices and sauces that would otherwise escape from the burritos, making them less messy and more flavorful. Liquids in burritos may also cause the tortilla to be soggy, falling apart as the burrito is eaten. So, don't skip the rice!

You could always use plain cooked rice in these recipes, but we suggest trying either version of rice—red or green—for added flavor (page 10).

Tortilla Preparation

All recipes call for thin, large flour tortillas with 12-inch diameters. Any variety or flavor can be used—such as tortillas with spinach or other flavorings.

It is essential to warm the tortillas before rolling burritos, because this will soften the tortillas and prevent them from splitting during rolling. There are several ways to heat tortillas—they can be grilled, heated over a stovetop flame, or wrapped in aluminum foil and then baked in a hot oven.

The quickest and easiest method is heating tortillas in a microwave oven on a large plate covered with a kitchen towel. The time needed varies according to microwave ovens and according to the size and thickness of the tortillas. A general rule is about 30 seconds on high for one tortilla. The goal is to have the tortillas softened only, and not crisped, so watch them closely and check frequently while cooking.

Homemade Flour Tortillas

3 cups all-purpose flour

1 teaspoon salt

1 teaspoon baking powder

1/3 cup lard, melted (for vegetarian tortillas, use vegetable oil)

1 cup hot water

If you're feeling a little more ambitious and have the time, homemade flour tortillas can't be beat. Here's our easy recipe.

Stir together all ingredients in a large bowl. Turn onto a lightly floured surface and knead for 1 minute. Place in an oiled bowl. Cover bowl with a large kitchen towel and let sit in a warm place for about 1 hour.

Make 12 balls of dough. Roll each ball out with a rolling pin on a lightly floured surface to 10–12 inches. Cook on a large griddle or skillet over medium-high heat until lightly browned on both sides.

☀ **Makes 12 large tortillas**

Mexican Green Rice

2 cups low-sodium chicken or vegetable broth

1 cup uncooked long-grain rice

Flesh of $1/2$ large ripe avocado

$1/2$ cup chopped fresh cilantro

$1/4$ cup green salsa or green hot sauce

Salt and freshly ground pepper, to taste

Bring broth to a boil in a medium saucepan over high heat. Add rice, cover, reduce heat to medium-low, and cook until rice is tender and liquid is absorbed, about 20 minutes. Fluff rice with a fork and let cool to warm. Blend in a blender the avocado, cilantro, and salsa, adding a little water as needed to blend smoothly, to the consistency of sour cream. Stir into rice. Season with salt and pepper.

☀ **Makes 3 cups**

Mexican Red Rice

3 tablespoons butter or vegetable oil

$1/2$ medium onion, minced

3 cloves garlic, pressed

1 cup uncooked long-grain white rice

$1^3/4$ cups low-sodium chicken or vegetable broth

$1/2$ cup Red Enchilada Sauce (page 124)

Salt and freshly ground pepper, to taste

Add oil to a medium saucepan over medium-high heat. Add onion and cook until translucent, 3–5 minutes. Add garlic and cook another minute. Add rice, stirring to coat each grain with oil. Whisk together the broth and enchilada sauce. Stir into rice. Cover and simmer over low heat until liquid is absorbed, 15–18 minutes. Remove from heat and let sit 10 minutes. Fluff with fork and add salt and pepper.

☀ **Makes 3 cups**

RISE
AND SHINE

CALIFORNIA DREAMIN'

4 ounces thin-sliced bacon

8 ounces frozen hash-brown potatoes

6 large eggs

2 tablespoons heavy cream

$1/2$ teaspoon salt

$1/4$ teaspoon pepper

2 tablespoons butter

4 to 6 (12-inch) flour tortillas, warmed

4 ounces cheddar cheese, grated

1 large ripe avocado, thinly sliced

4 to 6 tablespoons salsa

Slice bacon across the grain into $1/4$-inch pieces. Add bacon to cold skillet over medium heat and cook, stirring frequently, until browned and crispy, about 3 minutes. Remove bacon and leave fat in skillet.

Scatter potatoes in pan in a thin layer. Cook until lightly browned on bottom, about 5 minutes. Using a wide spatula, turn over hash browns and cook on other side until crispy, about 5 more minutes. Remove from skillet and wipe skillet clean with a paper towel.

Whisk together eggs, cream, salt, and pepper in a small bowl.

Melt butter in skillet over medium heat. Pour in egg mixture and use a spatula to push eggs into large clumps and turn eggs over and cook until eggs are solid, but not browned, about 7 minutes.

Assemble burritos by spooning eggs onto tortillas. Add potatoes, cheese, and bacon. Add avocado and salsa. Roll burritos as desired.

These are excellent served with sour cream spooned on top.

☀ **Makes 4 to 6 burritos**

DENVER OMELET

2 tablespoons butter

1 medium onion, diced

1/2 red bell pepper, seeded and diced

1/2 green bell pepper, seeded and diced

1 cup diced ham

8 large eggs

2 tablespoons sour cream

1 tablespoon cayenne pepper sauce

Salt and freshly ground pepper, to taste

1 (15-ounce) can refried beans, warmed

4 ounces cheddar cheese, grated

4 to 6 (12-inch) flour tortillas, warmed

Melt butter in a large skillet over medium-high heat. Cook onion and peppers until vegetables are softened and onions are translucent, about 7 minutes. Add ham and cook, about 2 minutes.

Reduce heat to medium-low. Whisk together eggs, sour cream, and cayenne pepper sauce in a small bowl. Add to skillet and stir occasionally, scraping bottom of skillet and forming large curds with the eggs. Cook just until eggs are set but not browned, about 7 minutes. Add salt and pepper.

Assemble burritos by spooning beans and cheese on tortillas. Top with egg mixture. Roll burritos as desired.

For a quick sauce that pairs well with this burrito, try adding 1 teaspoon minced chipotle pepper with adobo sauce into 1/2 cup ketchup.

☀ **Makes 4 to 6 burritos**

HASH BROWNS AND EGGS

2 tablespoons vegetable oil

1 poblano chile,* cut into matchstick pieces

16 ounces frozen hash-brown potatoes

Salt and freshly ground pepper, to taste

1 tablespoon butter

4 to 6 large eggs

1 (15-ounce) can refried beans, warmed

4 to 6 (12-inch) flour tortillas, warmed

3 green onions, white and green parts, thinly sliced

1 tomato, seeded and diced

4 ounces cheddar cheese, grated

Warm oil in a large skillet over medium-high heat. Add poblano and hash browns and cook until crispy and browned, turning occasionally, about 8 minutes. Transfer to a plate and wipe skillet with a paper towel.

Lower heat to medium-low. Melt butter and cook eggs in the butter until yolks are hard, turning over once. Remove eggs from skillet and cut into thin strips.

Assemble burritos by spreading beans onto tortillas. Add potato mixture, eggs, onions, tomato, and cheese. Roll burritos as desired.

* You may substitute other types of chiles here, such as an Anaheim or jalapeño, but keep in mind that poblanos are very mild and most other chiles have much more heat.

Serve with Red Enchilada Sauce (page 124) or Green Enchilada Sauce (page 125).

☀ **Makes 4 to 6 burritos**

CHORIZO AND POTATO

1 tablespoon vegetable oil

$3/4$ pound uncooked Mexican chorizo, casings removed

1 large russet potato, peeled and diced into $1/4$-inch cubes

$1/2$ large sweet onion, diced

3 cloves garlic, minced

1 teaspoon salt

1 tablespoon cayenne pepper sauce

$1 1/4$ cups refried beans, warmed

4 to 6 (12-inch) flour tortillas, warmed

4 ounces Monterey Jack or cheddar cheese, grated

4 green onions, white and green parts, thinly sliced

Warm oil in a large skillet over medium-high heat. Add chorizo, breaking it up into small bits and cook until lightly browned and cooked through, about 10 minutes. Remove chorizo from skillet, leaving fat in pan.

Add potato to skillet and cook, stirring constantly until fork tender, 3–5 minutes. Add onion and cook, stirring frequently, until onion is softened, about 3 minutes. Add garlic and cook until fragrant, about 1 minute. Add chorizo back into skillet. Season with salt and cayenne pepper sauce.

Assemble burritos by spooning refried beans and chorizo mixture onto tortillas. Sprinkle with cheese and green onions. Roll burritos as desired.

Tomatillo Cream Sauce (page 124) is a great way to finish this burrito.

☀ **Makes 4 to 6 burritos**

BUTTERNUT SQUASH AND APPLE HASH

4 cups 1/2-inch cubes peeled butternut squash

3 tablespoons vegetable oil

1 teaspoon cinnamon

1 teaspoon ground cumin

1/2 teaspoon chipotle powder

1/2 teaspoon smoked paprika

1 small onion, diced

1 Granny Smith apple, peeled, cored, and diced

Salt and freshly ground pepper, to taste

2 tablespoons butter

6 large eggs

2 tablespoons milk

4 to 6 (12-inch) flour tortillas, warmed

4 ounces Monterey Jack cheese, grated

Spread squash cubes evenly on a plate. Cook squash in a microwave until slightly softened but not cooked through, 3–4 minutes. Warm oil and spices in a large skillet over medium-high heat. Add squash and onion and cook until onion is translucent, about 8 minutes. Add apple and cook until squash is fork tender. Season with salt and pepper.

Melt butter in another medium skillet over medium heat. Whisk eggs and milk together with a pinch of salt and pepper and pour into skillet and scramble until eggs are soft curds, 3–5 minutes.

Assemble burritos by spooning squash mixture and eggs onto tortillas. Sprinkle with cheese. Roll burritos as desired.

Serve with a dollop of sour cream, guacamole, or salsa.

☀ **Makes 4 to 6 burritos**

RANCH BREAKFAST

12 ounces bacon, diced

1 medium onion, diced

1 pound frozen diced potatoes, thawed

Salt and freshly ground pepper, to taste

1 (4-ounce) can roasted green chiles, diced

4 to 6 large eggs

6 ounces cheddar cheese, grated

4 to 6 (12-inch) flour tortillas, warmed

Cook bacon in a large skillet over medium-high heat until crispy, about 8 minutes. Remove from pan and drain on paper towels. Drain bacon fat, leaving 3-4 tablespoons in pan. Add onion and cook until translucent, about 5 minutes. Stir in potatoes and cook until golden brown, about 10 minutes. Season with salt and pepper. Stir in green chiles.

With a spoon, make 4 to 6 indentations in top of potatoes, large enough to hold 1 egg. Crack 1 egg into each indentation. Sprinkle cheese evenly over top of potatoes and cover with a lid. Cook until egg whites are firm and yolks are runny.

Assemble burritos by scooping 1 egg and potato mixture onto tortillas. Sprinkle with bacon. Roll burritos as desired.

Red Enchilada Sauce (page 124) or salsa spooned over the top is a tasty addition to this burrito.

☀ **Makes 4 to 6 burritos**

HUEVOS EL DIABLO

6 plum tomatoes, halved

1 medium yellow onion, halved

3 jalapeños, stemmed and seeded, halved

4 tablespoons vegetable oil, divided

Salt and freshly ground pepper, to taste

4 cloves garlic, minced

1/2 teaspoon dried Mexican oregano

1/2 teaspoon red pepper flakes (optional)

4 to 6 large eggs

1 (15-ounce) can cannellini beans, drained and warmed

2 tablespoons butter

4 to 6 (12-inch) flour tortillas, warmed

4 ounces queso fresco, crumbled

3 tablespoons minced fresh cilantro

Preheat oven to broil.

Toss tomatoes, onion, and jalapeños with 2 table-spoons vegetable oil in a large bowl. Spread on a baking sheet, cut sides down, and season with salt and pepper. Broil until skins begin to turn dark brown, 6–8 minutes. Remove charred skins and pulse in a food processor to make a chunky sauce.

Heat remaining oil in a large skillet over medium-high heat. Add oregano, red pepper flakes, and garlic and then cook until fragrant. Add sauce to skillet and bring to a boil. Reduce heat to medium low and crack eggs into sauce, one at a time. Cook until eggs are desired doneness and season with salt and pepper.

Mash beans with a potato masher or fork, until chunky, then stir in butter until melted.

Assemble burritos by spooning beans on tortillas. Add 1 egg and sauce. Sprinkle with queso fresco and cilantro. Roll burritos as desired.

☀ **Makes 4 to 6 burritos**

UPDATED CLASSICS

CHILE VERDE

3 tablespoons vegetable oil

2 pounds pork shoulder, excess fat removed and cut into 2-inch chunks

1 1/2 cups diced yellow onion

4 cloves garlic, chopped

3 Anaheim chiles, roasted, stemmed and seeded, peeled, and diced

3 poblano chiles, roasted, stemmed and seeded, peeled, and diced

2 cups low-sodium chicken or vegetable broth

1 cup water

1 teaspoon dried Mexican oregano

1/2 teaspoon ground cumin

1 1/2 teaspoons salt

1 teaspoon freshly ground pepper

1 (15-ounce) can white beans, drained and warmed

4 to 6 (12-inch) flour tortillas, warmed

2 ounces Monterey Jack cheese, grated

Heat oil in a large heavy stockpot or Dutch oven over medium-high heat. Add pork and brown well on all sides. Add onion and cook until softened. Add garlic and cook 1-2 minutes more. Add chiles, broth, water, spices, salt, and pepper. Simmer, uncovered, over low heat until pork is tender and the liquid is thickened, stirring occasionally, about 1 hour.

Mash beans with a potato masher or fork, until chunky.

Assemble burritos by spooning beans onto tortillas. Add chile verde and sprinkle with cheese. Roll burritos as desired.

These are excellent served enchilada style with Tomatillo Cream Sauce (page 124) or Green Enchilada Sauce (page 125) and additional cheese melted on top.

☀ **Makes 4 to 6 burritos**

CARNE ASADA

3 limes

2 oranges

6 cloves garlic

1 large handful fresh cilantro

2 tablespoons white vinegar

3/4 cup olive oil

1 to 2 jalapeños, stemmed and seeded

2 pounds flank steak, skirt steak, or New York Strip

1 teaspoon salt

1/2 teaspoon freshly ground pepper

4 to 6 (12-inch) flour tortillas, warmed

1 1/2 cups guacamole

1 cup salsa or pico de gallo

1/2 cup cotija cheese, crumbled

Cut limes and oranges in half and remove seeds from oranges. Place, with peels, in a food processor. Add garlic, cilantro, vinegar, olive oil, and jalapeño and pulse to make a paste. Scrape paste into a ziplock bag. Add steak and cover completely in paste. Marinate in refrigerator for at least 4 hours and up to 8 hours.

Take steak out of marinade, scrape to remove excess paste, and transfer to a plate. Season both sides with salt and pepper.

Heat an outdoor grill or grill pan over medium-high heat. Grill steak until medium-rare, 7–9 minutes per side. Remove steak from grill and allow to rest, about 10 minutes. Slice steak across the grain into very thin strips then cut into smaller pieces.

Assemble burritos by dividing steak among tortillas. Add guacamole, salsa, and sprinkle with cheese. Roll burritos as desired.

These are excellent served enchilada style with Tomatillo Cream Sauce (page 124), Red Enchilada Sauce (page 124), or Red Chile Mole Sauce (page 122) and additional cheese melted on top.

☀ **Makes 4 to 6 burritos**

PORK AL PASTOR

2 to 3 dried chiles, such as guajillo or pasilla, stemmed and seeded

1/4 cup frozen orange juice concentrate

1/4 cup red wine vinegar

1/2 cup pineapple juice

3 cloves garlic, minced

1 teaspoon salt

1/2 teaspoon ground cumin

1/2 white onion, chopped

1 1/2 pounds boneless pork loin

2 tablespoons vegetable oil

1/2 ripe pineapple, peeled and cored

1 cup refried beans, warmed

4 to 6 (12-inch) flour tortillas, warmed

2 cups cooked long-grain white rice or Mexican Red Rice (page 10), warmed

3 green onions, white and green parts, thinly sliced

1 cup chopped fresh cilantro leaves

Chop chiles into pieces and add to a medium bowl. Cover with boiling water and let sit about 20 minutes, until softened.

Place softened chiles in food processor or blender with orange juice concentrate, vinegar, pineapple juice, garlic, salt, cumin, and onion. Blend until smooth.

Cut pork across the grain into 1-inch-thick slices. Heat oil in a large skillet over medium-high heat. Add pork in a single layer (you will need to cook in batches). Cook pork until lightly browned on both sides. Remove from skillet, transfer to a cutting board, and let cool. Cut pork into 1/4-inch strips.

Pour chile-orange juice mixture into skillet. Add pork and cook, stirring constantly, until sauce clings to pork and most of liquid has evaporated.

Cut pineapple into 1-inch slices and grill or broil until a little char appears on all sides, about 5 minutes. Let pineapple cool, dice, and set aside.

Assemble burritos by spooning beans onto tortillas. Add pork, rice, green onions, and cilantro. Roll burritos as desired.

☀ **Makes 4 to 6 burritos**

RED CHILE ADOBO BEEF

12 cloves garlic

2 teaspoons ground cumin

2 tablespoons dried Mexican oregano

2 bay leaves

1/8 teaspoon ground cloves

2 teaspoons freshly ground pepper

1/2 teaspoon ground canela or cinnamon

1 dried negro chile, stemmed and seeded

2 dried guajillo chiles, stemmed and seeded

3 dried ancho chiles, stemmed and seeded

4 cups fresh orange juice

2 tablespoons apple cider vinegar

2 tablespoons brown sugar

1 1/2 tablespoons salt

2 to 3 tablespoons vegetable oil

2 pounds beef chuck, cut into 2-inch cubes

4 to 6 (12-inch) flour tortillas, warmed

Preheat oven to 325 degrees. (Or, if using a slow cooker, preheat to low setting.)

Heat a Dutch oven or large skillet over medium-high heat. Add garlic and cook until golden brown on all sides, about 4 minutes. Add spices to skillet and toast until warm and fragrant, 2–3 minutes. Add chiles to skillet and toast lightly. Add orange juice, vinegar, brown sugar, and salt. Simmer until chiles are soft. Remove from heat and set aside to cool. Pour into a blender and purée until smooth.

Heat oil in a Dutch oven or large skillet over medium-high heat. Season beef with salt and pepper. Brown beef on all sides, in batches, and drain on paper towels. Return beef to Dutch oven or place in slow cooker.

Pour blender mixture over beef. Cover and bake or cook in slow cooker until beef is tender and shreds apart, about 2 hours.

Assemble burritos by spooning beef mixture onto tortillas. Roll into burritos.

☀ **Makes 4 to 6 burritos**

CHICKEN TINGA

1 tablespoon vegetable oil

1/2 large sweet onion, diced

2 cloves garlic, minced

1 large tomatillo, diced

1 teaspoon ground cumin

1 teaspoon dried Mexican oregano

1 teaspoon salt

1 (15-ounce) can fire-roasted diced tomatoes, with liquid

2 chipotle chiles in adobo sauce, minced

1 tablespoon cayenne pepper sauce

4 cups large chunked cooked chicken

1 (15-ounce) can black or pinto beans, drained and rinsed

4 to 6 (12-inch) flour tortillas, warmed

4 ounces cheddar cheese, grated

Heat oil in a large skillet over medium-high heat. Add onion and cook until softened, about 3 minutes. Add garlic and cook for 1 minute. Add tomatillo, cumin, oregano, and salt and cook, stirring constantly, another 3 minutes. Add tomatoes, chipotles, and cayenne pepper sauce, and let cook until most of liquid has evaporated. Remove from heat and let cool to warm. Purée in blender until smooth.

Add mixture back into skillet over medium-low heat and bring to a simmer. Stir in chicken and let cook, stirring occasionally and gently, until sauce clings to chicken and most of liquid has evaporated.

Mash beans with a potato masher or fork, until chunky.

Assemble burritos by spooning chicken mixture onto tortillas. Add beans and sprinkle with cheese. Roll burritos as desired.

Sour cream or Tomatillo Cream Sauce (page 124) will complement the flavors of this burrito.

☀ **Makes 4 to 6 burritos**

DOUBLE-ROLLED BEAN AND CHEESE

8 ounces cheddar cheese, grated, divided

3 green onions, white and green parts, thinly sliced

4 ounces sour cream

2 1/2 cups refried pinto or black beans

1/4 cup minced white onion

1/4 cup salsa or pico de gallo

2 tablespoons cayenne pepper sauce

4 to 6 (12-inch) flour tortillas, warmed

4 to 6 (6- to 8-inch) flour tortillas, warmed

2 ounces queso fresco, crumbled*

Place 6 ounces cheddar cheese in a mixing bowl. Stir in green onions and sour cream.

Place remaining cheddar cheese in medium saucepan over medium heat. Add refried beans, onions, salsa, and cayenne pepper sauce. Cook, stirring constantly, until bubbly, about 8 minutes.

Assemble burritos by spooning about 3/4 cup bean mixture onto center of each 12-inch tortilla. Sprinkle queso fresco onto beans. Place small tortillas onto queso fresco. Spoon cheddar cheese mixture down center in a line about 2 inches wide. When finished, you will have a center core of the cheese mixture surrounded by a layer of refried beans. Roll burritos using the Traditional Rolled Burrito method (page 4) so that cheese mixture forms a center core.

* A good substitute for queso fresco is feta cheese.

Salsa or diced tomatoes and onions would be tasty toppings for this burrito.

☀ **Makes 4 to 6 burritos**

MAYAN SHREDDED PORK

6 tablespoons achiote paste

2 cups fresh orange juice, divided

1/2 cup fresh lime juice

2 teaspoons apple cider vinegar, divided

2 cloves garlic, minced

1/2 teaspoon dried Mexican oregano

1/4 teaspoon ground cumin

2 pounds boneless pork shoulder

1 teaspoon salt

1/4 teaspoon freshly ground pepper

1 large banana leaf (found at Latin or Asian markets), optional

2 cups water

1 red onion, thinly sliced

4 to 6 (12-inch) flour tortillas, warmed

1 cup salsa or pico de gallo

1/2 cup minced fresh cilantro

In a large glass bowl, mix achiote paste, 1 1/2 cups orange juice, lime juice, 1 teaspoon vinegar, garlic, oregano, and cumin together. Trim excess fat from pork. Place pork in bowl and coat in marinade. Cover and let marinate in refrigerator for at least 4 hours or overnight, turning occasionally.

Preheat oven to 375 degrees.

Remove pork from marinade. Season pork with salt and pepper. Place pork in a Dutch oven lined with banana leaf, if using. Add marinade and water. Wrap leaf over top of pork and cover with lid or aluminum foil.

Place pork in oven and bake for 20 minutes. Reduce heat to 300 degrees and cook until pork shreds apart, 6–8 hours, removing lid during the last hour of cooking.

Toward the end of cooking time, rinse onions in very hot water then soak in remaining orange juice and remaining vinegar for 1–2 hours.

Assemble burritos by placing shredded pork onto tortillas with tongs or a fork so that excess liquid drains away. Add desired amount of salsa, cilantro, and pickled red onions. Roll burritos as desired.

☀ **Makes 4 to 6 burritos**

ARROZ CON POLLO

2 tablespoons taco seasoning

1 1/2 teaspoons salt, divided

3/4 teaspoon freshly ground pepper, divided

1 to 2 tablespoons water

4 boneless, skinless chicken thighs or breasts

12 ounces bacon, diced

1 yellow onion, chopped

2 cloves garlic, minced

1 green bell pepper, seeded and chopped

2 bay leaves

1 1/2 cups long-grain white rice

1 (15-ounce) can diced tomatoes, with liquid

2 1/4 cups low-sodium chicken broth

2 tablespoons apple cider vinegar

4 to 6 (12-inch) flour tortillas, warmed

1/2 cup sliced pimiento-stuffed green olives

1 cup salsa verde

Preheat oven to 350 degrees.

In a small bowl, mix taco seasoning, 1/2 teaspoon salt, and 1/4 teaspoon pepper with water to make a paste. Rub each piece of chicken with spice paste and refrigerate for 30 minutes.

Cook bacon in a large Dutch oven over medium-high heat until crispy. Remove bacon with a slotted spoon, leaving bacon fat in pan.

Place chicken in pan and brown on all sides. Remove chicken and set aside. Add onion, garlic, bell pepper, and bay leaves and cook until softened, about 5 minutes. Stir in rice and stir until well coated and translucent, about 2 minutes.

Pour in tomatoes, chicken broth, and vinegar. Season with remaining salt and pepper. Return bacon and chicken to pan and bring to a boil over high heat, reduce heat to medium-low and simmer for 5 minutes. Cover and bake until chicken is cooked and the liquid has been absorbed, 20–25 minutes.

Assemble burritos by shredding chicken and spooning onto tortillas. Garnish with green olives and salsa verde. Roll burritos as desired.

For a different topping, try Green Enchilada Sauce (page 125).

☀ **Makes 4 to 6 burritos**

CHICKEN MOLE

4 cups large chunks shredded cooked chicken

1 recipe Red Chile Mole (page 122), warmed

1/2 small onion, diced

2 tablespoons butter

2 cloves garlic, minced

1 (15-ounce) can black beans, drained and rinsed

Salt and freshly ground pepper, to taste

3 cups cooked long-grain white rice or Mexican Green Rice, (page 10)

4 to 6 (12-inch) flour tortillas, warmed

1 1/2 cups grated cheddar or longhorn cheese

Heat chicken and mole in medium saucepan over medium heat. Bring mixture to a simmer and cook until chicken is heated through, 8–10 minutes. Add a little water if mole becomes too thick.

Cook onion in butter over medium heat in another medium saucepan until soft. Add garlic and cook for 2 more minutes. Add beans and heat. Mash beans with a potato masher or fork, until chunky. Season with salt and pepper.

Assemble burritos by spooning bean mixture and rice onto tortillas. Add chicken mole. Sprinkle with cheese and roll burritos as desired.

These are excellent served enchilada style with additional mole over the burritos and additional cheese melted on top.

☀ **Makes 4 to 6 burritos**

TEQUILA SUNRISE CHICKEN AND PEPPERS

1/2 cup tequila

1 cup fresh orange juice

Zest and juice of 1 lime

6 green onions, white and green parts, thinly sliced, divided

4 tablespoons vegetable oil, divided

1 teaspoon salt

2 large boneless, skinless chicken breasts

1 medium onion

1 red bell pepper

1 yellow bell pepper

2 1/2 cups refried beans

4 to 6 (12-inch) flour tortillas, warmed

2 ounces Monterey Jack or cheddar cheese, grated

Whisk together tequila, orange juice, lime zest and juice, half of green onions, 1 tablespoon oil, and salt in a small bowl. Pour into a ziplock bag, add chicken, and squeeze with hands to evenly distribute the marinade. Refrigerate 2–4 hours. Let stand at room temperature for 30 minutes before cooking.

Remove chicken from bag and blot dry with paper towels. Pour marinade into small saucepan. Bring to a boil, and then reduce to a simmer over medium-low heat until thickened, 3–5 minutes.

Toss chicken with 2 tablespoons oil. Cook on an outdoor grill or grill pan over medium-high heat until cooked through, 3–5 minutes per side. While chicken is cooking, brush generously with marinade on both sides, using all of the marinade. Remove chicken from heat and let rest 10 minutes. Cut chicken across grain into 1/4-inch slices.

Slice onion and bell peppers into 1/4-inch-thick slices. Toss with remaining oil. Grill on an outdoor grill or grill pan over high heat until lightly charred and tender-crisp.

Assemble burritos by spooning beans on tortillas. Add chicken, vegetables, remaining green onions, and cheese. Roll burritos as desired.

☀ **Makes 4 to 6 burritos**

OLD WORLD POSOLE

2 pounds boneless pork shoulder

$1/2$ cup Coca Cola (not diet)

$1/2$ cup fresh orange juice

2 teaspoons ground cumin

3 tablespoons chile powder

$1^1/2$ medium yellow onions, chopped, divided

3 cloves garlic, minced

1 cup low-sodium chicken or vegetable broth

1 (15-ounce) can hominy, drained

2 cups cooked long-grain white rice or Mexican Green Rice (page 10), warmed

4 to 6 (12-inch) flour tortillas, warmed

$1/4$ cup chopped fresh cilantro

$1/4$ cup radishes, cut into thin matchsticks (optional)

Cut pork into 4 pieces and place in slow cooker.

Combine Coca Cola, orange juice, cumin, and chile powder in small bowl and pour over pork. Add $2/3$ onions and garlic. Pour in broth and cover. Cook on low until pork is tender and can be pulled apart with a fork, 6–8 hours.

Remove pork from slow cooker, allow to cool enough to handle, then shred. Add hominy to slow cooker and continue to cook until hominy is hot.

Assemble burritos by spooning rice and pork onto tortillas. With a slotted spoon, scoop hominy from slow cooker and spoon over pork. Garnish with cilantro, radishes, and remaining onion. Roll burritos as desired.

☀ **Makes 4 to 6 burritos**

SLOW-COOKER MACHACA BEEF

3 pounds chuck roast, cut into 2-inch cubes

1½ teaspoons salt

¾ teaspoon freshly ground pepper

¼ cup New Mexico red chile powder

2 teaspoons ground cumin

4 cloves garlic, minced

2 (4-ounce) cans diced green chiles

1 medium yellow onion, thinly sliced

1 green bell pepper, seeded and thinly sliced

4 to 6 (12-inch) flour tortillas, warmed

4 ounces cheddar cheese, grated

1 cup pico de gallo or salsa

Toss beef with salt, spices, garlic, and green chiles in a large bowl. Place in a slow cooker. Cook 8–10 hours on low.

Remove meat and juices from slow cooker, place in sealed container, and chill in refrigerator until meat cools and fat floats to top and becomes hardened. Skim off fat and discard.

Cook onion and bell pepper in a large skillet over medium heat. Using tongs so liquid drains away from meat, add meat to skillet, and cook until heated through. With a fork, gently pull apart or shred meat as it is cooking. Add leftover juices if meat becomes too dry.

Assemble burritos by spooning meat mixture onto tortillas. Add cheese and pico de gallo. Roll burritos as desired.

☀ **Makes 4 to 6 burritos**

NEW SOUTH
OF THE BORDER

TEQUILA LIME SHRIMP

1/4 cup tequila

Zest and juice of 3 limes

Zest and juice of 1 orange

1 teaspoon ground cumin

1 to 2 jalapeños, stemmed and seeded, minced, divided

3 cloves garlic, minced, divided

2 pounds uncooked medium shrimp, peeled and deveined

Salt and freshly ground pepper, to taste

2 to 3 tablespoons vegetable oil

1 recipe Mexican Green Rice (page 10), warmed

4 to 6 (12-inch) flour tortillas, warmed

1 recipe Chimichurri Sauce (page 125) or bottled salsa verde

Mix tequila, lime juice, orange juice, 1 teaspoon each of zests, cumin, 1/3 jalapeño, and 1 clove garlic in a large ziplock bag. Add shrimp and marinate for 1 hour in refrigerator.

Remove shrimp from refrigerator and drain, reserving 1/4 cup of marinade. Season shrimp with salt and pepper. Heat oil in a large skillet over medium-high heat. Place shrimp and remaining jalapeño and garlic in skillet, cook 1–2 minutes. Add reserved marinade and cook until liquid has reduced and shrimp are cooked through and pink, 2–3 minutes.

Assemble burritos by spooning rice onto tortillas. Add shrimp and drizzle with Chimichurri Sauce or salsa verde. Roll burritos as desired.

Guacamole would be a perfect addition to this burrito.

☀ **Makes 4 to 6 burritos**

CANCUN GRILLED CHICKEN

4 boneless, skinless chicken breasts

2 (1-ounce) packages taco seasoning

2 cups fresh orange juice, divided

2 tablespoons fresh lime juice or apple cider vinegar

1/4 cup olive oil

1 red onion, thinly sliced, divided

2 cloves garlic, minced

1 habañero or jalapeño, stemmed and seeded, minced

1 teaspoon salt

Salt and freshly ground pepper, to taste

4 to 6 fresh or canned pineapple rings

2 cups cooked long-grain white rice or Mexican Green Rice (page 10), warmed

1 (15-ounce) can Ranch Style Beans, drained and warmed

4 to 6 (12-inch) flour tortillas, warmed

Guacamole, shredded lettuce, salsa, and sour cream

Rub both sides of chicken breasts with taco seasoning and place in a ziplock bag.

Combine 1 1/2 cups orange juice, lime juice, oil, any remaining taco seasoning, 1/4 onion, garlic, and habañero and add to the bag. Refrigerate 24 hours.

Rinse the remaining onion in boiling water. Place in a small bowl. Add remaining orange juice and 1 teaspoon salt. Set aside to pickle onions. Drain before serving.

Remove chicken from refrigerator 30 minutes before grilling. Remove chicken from marinade and season with salt and pepper on both sides. Grill on an outdoor grill or grill pan over medium-high heat until cooked, 10–12 minutes on each side. To insure even cooking, place a metal pie plate over chicken. Transfer to a plate and let rest 10 minutes. Slice into 1/2-inch-thick strips.

Grill the pineapple on each side until grill marks appear, about 6 minutes total. Transfer to a plate and let rest. Cut each ring in half.

Assemble burritos by spooning rice and beans on tortillas. Add chicken, pineapple, guacamole, lettuce, salsa, sour cream, and pickled onions. Roll burritos as desired.

☀ **Makes 4 to 6 burritos**

BLACK BEAN, CORN, AND QUINOA

2 tablespoons vegetable oil

1 medium sweet white onion, diced

1 red bell pepper, diced

1 jalapeño, stemmed and seeded, diced

2 teaspoons chile powder

1 teaspoon ground cumin

2 cups vegetable broth

1 tablespoon cayenne pepper sauce

1 cup quinoa

1 (15-ounce) can black beans, drained and rinsed

1 cup fresh or frozen thawed corn

1/4 cup minced fresh cilantro

Salt and freshly ground pepper, to taste

4 to 6 (12-inch) flour tortillas, warmed

2 ounces Monterey Jack cheese, grated

Heat oil in a large skillet over medium-high heat. Add onion, pepper, jalapeño, chile powder, and cumin and stir. Cook until vegetables are softened, 3–5 minutes.

Stir in broth, cayenne pepper sauce, and quinoa and bring to a boil. Reduce to a simmer, cover, and cook until quinoa is cooked and all liquid has evaporated, about 20 minutes.

Mash beans with a potato masher or fork, until chunky. Stir beans, corn, and cilantro into skillet mixture. Add salt and pepper.

Assemble burritos by spooning skillet mixture onto tortillas and sprinkling with cheese. Roll burritos as desired.

Any of the sauces from this cookbook will pair well with the veggie abundance in this burrito.

☼ **Makes 4 to 6 burritos**

SPICY GRILLED SALMON WITH CITRUS

1 (11-ounce) can mandarin oranges, drained and chopped

1 avocado, diced

2 tablespoons finely diced red onion

1/2 cup Chimichurri Sauce (page 125) or bottled salsa verde

4 (6-ounce) salmon fillets

1/2 cup vegetable oil, divided

2 teaspoons smoked paprika

1 teaspoon chipotle powder

1 teaspoon ground cumin

1/4 teaspoon onion powder

1/4 teaspoon garlic powder

1/2 teaspoon salt

1/4 teaspoon freshly ground pepper

1 teaspoon sugar

1 recipe Mexican Green Rice (page 10), warmed

4 to 6 (12-inch) flour tortillas, warmed

Toss oranges, avocado, and onion with Chimichurri Sauce in medium bowl. Cover and set aside.

Brush both sides of salmon with oil. Mix spices and sugar in a small bowl. Place salmon on a plate and sprinkle spice mixture over salmon, lightly coating both sides. Heat an outdoor grill or grill pan over medium-high heat and brush with oil. Grill salmon until golden brown on outside and nearly opaque in the center, 3-4 minutes on each side. Transfer to plate to rest. Flake salmon into chunks.

Assemble burritos by spooning rice onto tortillas. Add salmon and orange-avocado mixture. Roll burritos as desired.

A little Green Enchilada Sauce (page 125) would be perfect on this burrito—with some melted cheese on top.

☀ **Makes 4 to 6 burritos**

ROASTED BEETS AND GOAT CHEESE

2 to 3 large beets (16 ounces total), with greens reserved

1 large white onion, diced

2 tablespoons olive oil

1 teaspoon salt

1 tablespoon chile powder

1 to 2 tablespoons cayenne pepper sauce

1 (15-ounce) can cannellini beans, rinsed, drained, and warmed

4 to 6 (12-inch) flour tortillas, warmed

2 ounces goat cheese, crumbled

2 ounces Monterey Jack cheese, grated

3 tablespoons minced cilantro

$1/2$ cup diced, toasted walnuts

Preheat oven to 425 degrees.

Wrap beets in aluminum foil and place on a baking sheet. Bake until beets are fork-tender, about 1 hour. Let cool to warm. Peel and dice beets into $1/2$-inch cubes.

Cook onion in oil in a large skillet over medium-high heat until softened, 3–5 minutes. Add salt, chile powder, cayenne pepper sauce, and beets. Cook until mixture is hot, 5–7 minutes. Remove stems and any brown spots from beet greens. Coarsely chop greens, add to skillet, and cook until wilted, about 3 minutes.

Mash beans with a potato masher or fork, until chunky.

Assemble burritos by spooning beet mixture onto tortillas. Add beans, cheeses, cilantro, and walnuts. Roll burritos as desired.

☀ **Makes 4 to 6 burritos**

TWICE-BARBECUED CHICKEN

4 cups water

1½ tablespoons salt

¼ cup plus 1 tablespoon brown sugar, divided

5 cloves garlic, minced, divided

4 sprigs fresh thyme

6 boneless, skinless chicken breasts

1 large mango, peeled and diced, or ¾ cup frozen

1 to 2 habañeros, stemmed and seeded

½ teaspoon salt, plus more to taste

¼ teaspoon pepper, plus more to taste

2 cups mild barbecue sauce

¼ cup vegetable oil

4 to 6 (12-inch) flour tortillas, warmed

¼ cup finely sliced green onions

8 ounces Monterey Jack or American cheese, grated

½ cup sour cream

Combine water, 1½ tablespoons salt, ¼ cup brown sugar, 2 cloves garlic, and thyme in a large pot. Add chicken and brine in refrigerator for up to 2 hours.

Blend in a blender, mango, habañero, remaining garlic, remaining brown sugar, ½ teaspoon salt, and ¼ teaspoon pepper. Pour into large saucepan over high heat, stir in barbecue sauce, and bring to boil. Reduce heat to medium-low and simmer for 5 minutes. Turn off heat and cover to keep warm.

Remove chicken from brine, pat dry, and season with salt and pepper on both sides.

Heat an outdoor grill or grill pan to medium heat and brush grill with oil. Grill chicken until almost cooked, turning only once, 10–12 minutes per side. Place a metal pie tin or aluminum foil over chicken to insure even cooking. Brush chicken on both sides with mango barbecue sauce and grill until chicken is cooked completely through, 1–2 minutes more. Set chicken aside to rest for 5 minutes. Dice chicken.

Spoon chicken onto tortillas. Drizzle with mango barbecue sauce, sprinkle with green onions and cheese. Roll burritos as desired and secure with toothpicks. Return burritos to grill and toast tortilla on each side creating grill marks. Remove toothpicks. Spoon barbecue sauce over burritos, garnish with sour cream, green onions, and cheese.

☀ **Makes 4 to 6 burritos**

SMOKY CARAMELIZED BUTTERNUT SQUASH

1 cup quinoa

3 cups low-sodium vegetable broth

1 large butternut squash, peeled

2 tablespoons butter or vegetable oil

2 tablespoons smoked paprika

1 tablespoon ground cumin

2 teaspoons brown sugar

1 tablespoon cayenne pepper sauce

4 to 6 (12-inch) flour tortillas, warmed

3 green onions, white and green parts, thinly sliced

2 tablespoons minced fresh cilantro

4 ounces Monterey Jack or cheddar cheese, grated

Bring quinoa and vegetable broth to a boil in a medium saucepan over high heat. Reduce to a simmer, cover, and cook until all broth has been absorbed and quinoa has burst, about 20 minutes. Uncover and let sit 5 minutes. Fluff with a fork.

Meanwhile, grate squash on large holes of a box grater or finely dice. (You should have 4 cups of grated squash.) Add butter, paprika, and cumin to a large skillet over medium-high heat. Cook until fragrant, 1–2 minutes. Add squash, brown sugar, and cayenne pepper sauce and cook, stirring frequently, until squash is lightly browned and fork tender, 5–8 minutes. Stir cooked quinoa into squash mixture and cook until all liquid evaporates, about 3 minutes.

Assemble burritos by spooning quinoa-squash mixture onto tortillas and sprinkle on the green onions, cilantro, and cheese. Roll burritos as desired.

☀ **Makes 4 to 6 burritos**

TRIPLE MUSHROOM AND SPINACH

1 medium yellow onion, diced

4 tablespoons vegetable oil, divided

3 cloves garlic, minced

2 teaspoons salt, divided

8 ounces cremini mushrooms, thinly sliced

8 ounces shiitake mushroom caps, thinly sliced

1 1/4 cups refried beans, warmed

2 large portobello mushroom caps

16 ounces spinach leaves, coarse stems discarded, chopped

1 tablespoon fresh lemon juice

4 to 6 (12-inch) flour tortillas, warmed

2 green onions, white and green parts, thinly sliced

2 ounces pepper jack cheese, grated

Cook onion and 2 tablespoons oil in a large skillet over medium-high heat, stirring until softened, about 3 minutes. Add garlic and 1 teaspoon salt and cook, 1 more minute. Add cremini and shiitake mushrooms and cook, stirring constantly until mushrooms are softened, about 5 minutes. Turn off heat and add remaining salt. Process mushrooms in a food processor and pulse until mushrooms are in small bits, but not puréed. Stir mushroom mixture into refried beans in a large bowl.

Brush portobello mushrooms with 1 tablespoon oil and cook in a large skillet over medium-high heat until lightly brown, about 5 minutes. Transfer to a cutting surface to cool then cut into 1/4-inch slices.

Wipe out skillet with paper towel and add remaining oil. Heat skillet over medium-high heat. Add spinach and cook until wilted, stirring frequently. Add in lemon juice, stirring so that liquid evaporates, about 2 minutes.

Assemble burritos by spooning mushroom-bean mixture onto tortillas. Add portobello slices, spinach, green onions, and cheese. Roll burritos as desired.

☀ Makes 4 to 6 burritos

SPICY CRISPY SHRIMP WITH MANGO

1 large avocado, peeled and diced

Zest and juice of 1 orange

1 large ripe mango, peeled and diced

1 small red onion, diced

Salt and freshly ground pepper, to taste

2 teaspoons honey

1 tablespoon minced chipotle in adobo

1/2 cup mayonnaise

1/2 teaspoon salt

1 clove garlic, minced

1 1/2 pounds frozen battered shrimp (without tails)

3 cups cooked long-grain white rice or Mexican Green Rice (page 10), warmed

4 to 6 (12-inch) flour tortillas, warmed

1/2 cup Mexican crema or sour cream

Diced mango or mango salsa

Toss avocado with orange juice in a small bowl until avocado is well coated. Add mango, onion, and orange zest and combine. Season with salt and pepper. Cover with plastic wrap, making sure plastic touches surface of salsa so avocado does not brown.

Mix honey, chipotle, and mayonnaise in a small bowl. Sprinkle 1/2 teaspoon salt over garlic on a cutting board and mash into a paste with the side of a knife or back of a spoon. Stir into mayonnaise mixture. Set aside.

Fry or bake shrimp until crispy according to the package directions. Drain on paper towels.

Working in batches, spread a few spoonfuls of spicy mayonnaise into a large mixing bowl and spread it around the sides. Add a batch of warm shrimp to the bowl and quickly toss to coat the shrimp and remove immediately. Repeat until all shrimp are coated.

Assemble burritos by spooning rice onto tortillas. Add shrimp and mango salsa. Roll burritos as desired. Garnish with crema and mango or mango salsa.

☀ **Makes 4 to 6 burritos**

CAULIFLOWER RICE AND POBLANO

1/2 red bell pepper, seeded

1 poblano chile, seeded

4 tablespoons olive oil, divided

1 small head cauliflower, core removed and cut into florets

1 tablespoon smoked paprika

1 teaspoon ground cumin

1 teaspoon salt

1 tablespoon cayenne pepper sauce

1 (15-ounce) can black refried beans, warmed

4 to 6 (12-inch) flour tortillas, warmed

1 ripe avocado, peeled and sliced

3 green onions, white and green parts, thinly sliced

Cut bell pepper and poblano into 2-inch-long and 1/4-inch-wide julienne strips.

Heat a large skillet over medium-high heat. Add 2 tablespoons of oil to skillet. Cook pepper and chile until softened and browned, 2–3 minutes. Remove from skillet and let cool.

Process cauliflower in a food processor in two batches until it is in small bits about the size of petite peas, 8–10 pulses. Measure about 4 cups, and save any remainder for another use. Add remaining oil to skillet, add paprika, and cook for 1 minute. Add cauliflower and cook, stirring constantly, until cauliflower is softened, 3–5 minutes. Add cumin, salt, and cayenne pepper sauce, stirring constantly to remove moisture, and cook another 3 minutes.

Assemble burritos by spooning beans onto tortillas. Add skillet mixture, avocado, and green onions. Roll burritos as desired.

Green Enchilada Sauce (page 125) would be an excellent topping—or a dollop of sour cream.

☀ **Makes 4 to 6 burritos**

BAJA SEAFOOD

2 tablespoons olive oil

1 shallot, minced

1 clove garlic, minced

1 jalapeño, stemmed and seeded, minced

1 pound uncooked small shrimp, peeled and deveined

8 ounces small scallops

1 teaspoon salt, divided

1/2 teaspoon pepper, divided

1/4 cup dry white wine

2 cups Tomatillo Cream Sauce (page 124)

2 cups cooked long-grain white rice or Mexican Green Rice (page 10), warmed

4 to 6 (12-inch) flour tortillas, warmed

1 large ripe avocado, sliced (optional)

3 ounces queso fresco, crumbled

Heat oil in a skillet over medium-high heat. Add shallot, garlic, and jalapeño and cook until softened, 1–2 minutes.

Season shrimp and scallops with 1/2 teaspoon salt and 1/4 teaspoon pepper. Add shrimp and scallops to skillet and sear on one side, 3–4 minutes. Turn shrimp and scallops over.

Add wine and simmer until wine is almost evaporated, about 3 minutes. Add Tomatillo Cream Sauce and bring to a simmer. Season with remaining salt and pepper.

Assemble burritos by spooning rice onto tortillas. Add shrimp-scallop mixture, avocado, if using, and cheese. Roll burritos as desired.

☀ **Makes 4 to 6 burritos**

MUSHROOM FAJITAS

1/2 cup red wine vinegar

1/2 cup Worcestershire sauce

1/2 cup olive oil

1/4 cup fresh lime juice

1/4 cup low-sodium soy sauce

1/2 cup chopped fresh cilantro

3 tablespoons minced garlic, divided

2 tablespoons minced jalapeño

6 large portobello mushroom caps

3/4 white onion, finely sliced

1 large poblano, stemmed and seeded, finely sliced

1 large red bell pepper, stemmed and seeded, finely sliced

Salt and freshly ground pepper, to taste

1 (15-ounce) can black or pinto beans, drained and warmed

4 to 6 (12-inch) flour tortillas, warmed

1 cup crumbled cotija cheese or queso fresco

Chimichurri Sauce (page 125)

Add vinegar, Worcestershire sauce, oil, lime juice, soy sauce, cilantro, 2 tablespoons garlic, and jalapeño to a ziplock bag. Cut mushrooms in half, place in marinade, and let sit for 1 hour. Remove mushrooms from marinade and slice into 1/4-inch-wide strips.

Cook mushrooms with onion, poblano, bell pepper, and remaining garlic over medium-high heat, until they are barely tender. Pour marinade over mushroom mixture and cook, 1–2 minutes more. Season with salt and pepper.

Assemble burritos by spooning beans onto tortillas. Add mushroom mixture, cheese, and Chimichurri Sauce. Roll burritos as desired.

☀ **Makes 4 to 6 burritos**

SOUTHWEST TOFU

3 tablespoons low-sodium soy sauce

1 tablespoon creamy peanut butter, or other nut butter

1 teaspoon ground cumin

1 teaspoon garlic powder

1 teaspoon chile powder

1 teaspoon cayenne pepper sauce

1 (16-ounce) package frozen and then thawed extra-firm tofu

2 tablespoons olive or vegetable oil

4 to 6 (12-inch) flour tortillas, warmed

2 (15-ounce) cans pinto or black beans, drained and warmed

3 green onions, white and green parts, thinly sliced

1 tomato, seeded and diced

4 ounces cheddar cheese, grated

Preheat oven to 350 degrees.

Mix soy sauce, peanut butter, spices, and cayenne pepper sauce in a medium bowl and set aside. Wrap tofu block in a thin kitchen towel and squeeze over sink until most of water is removed. Unwrap tofu and crumble into small bits into bowl and toss with soy sauce mixture.

Spread oil on a 12 x 18-inch baking sheet. Sprinkle tofu onto prepared sheet in a single layer. Bake 20 minutes. Remove from oven and stir tofu. Return to oven and bake until tofu is crispy, about 20 more minutes.

Mash beans with a potato masher or fork until chunky.

Assemble burritos by spooning tofu mixture onto tortillas. Add beans, onions, tomato, and cheese. Roll burritos as desired.

A dollop of guacamole and some diced tomatoes and cilantro would be excellent on this veggie burrito.

☼ **Makes 4 to 6 burritos**

ALL-AMERICAN CLASSICS

NEW ORLEANS RED BEANS AND RICE

2 tablespoons vegetable oil

1/2 cup minced onion

3 cloves garlic, minced

16 ounces andouille sausage, thinly cut
into half-moon slices

3 (15-ounce) cans red kidney beans, drained

3 cups low-sodium chicken or vegetable broth

2 tablespoons cayenne pepper sauce

Salt and freshly ground pepper, to taste

3 cups cooked long-grain white rice, warmed

4 to 6 (12-inch) flour tortillas, warmed

2 ounces Monterey Jack or pepper jack
cheese, grated

Add oil, onion, garlic, and sausage to large pot or Dutch oven over medium-high heat. Cook until onion is translucent, about 5 minutes.

Mash 1 can beans with a potato masher or fork, until chunky. Add mashed and unmashed beans, broth, and cayenne pepper sauce to the stockpot.* Reduce heat to low and simmer until mixture is the consistency of a thick gravy, stirring frequently, 20–30 minutes. Add salt and pepper.

Assemble burritos by spooning rice onto tortillas. Add red bean mixture and sprinkle on cheese. Roll burritos as desired.

* You can make this in a slow cooker at this point by cooking for 3–4 hours on high or 6–8 hours on low.

☀ Makes 4 to 6 burritos

CAJUN JAMBALAYA

2 tablespoons vegetable oil

2 boneless, skinless chicken thighs

4 ounces andouille sausage, cut into small pieces

1 small sweet onion, diced

1 green bell pepper, seeded and diced

2 teaspoons Cajun spice blend

3 cloves garlic, minced

$1/2$ cup long-grain white rice

$1 1/2$ cups low-sodium chicken or vegetable broth

1 tablespoon cayenne pepper sauce

1 (15-ounce) can diced tomatoes

8 ounces fresh or frozen okra, thawed and sliced into $1/2$-inch slices

6 medium uncooked shrimp, peeled, deveined, and chopped

2 tablespoons minced parsley

Salt and freshly ground pepper, to taste

4 to 6 (12-inch) flour tortillas, warmed

4 ounces Monterey Jack cheese, grated

Warm oil in a large skillet over medium-high heat. Add chicken and let cook until brown and cooked through, 3–5 minutes on each side. Transfer chicken to plate and let cool. Cut chicken into small pieces.

Add sausage, onion, bell pepper, and Cajun spice to skillet over medium-high heat. Cook until vegetables are softened, 2–3 minutes. Add garlic and rice and cook until rice is translucent, about 2 minutes. Add chicken broth, cayenne pepper sauce, tomatoes, and okra. Reduce heat to medium-low, cover, and cook 15 minutes. Add chicken and stir to combine. Cook until most of liquid has been absorbed and rice is tender, 6–8 minutes. Add shrimp and parsley to skillet, turn off heat, and season with salt and pepper. Cover and let rest, about 5 minutes.

Assemble burritos by spooning skillet mixture onto tortillas and sprinkle on cheese. Roll burritos as desired.

☀ **Makes 4 to 6 burritos**

SOUTHERN FRIED CHICKEN

1 cup low-sodium chicken or vegetable broth

1 cup yellow coarse grits

1/2 cup milk

1/2 cup grated pepper jack cheese

Salt and freshly ground pepper, to taste

8 ounces bacon, cooked and diced

6 boneless, skinless chicken breasts

1 cup all-purpose flour

1 (1-ounce) packet ranch seasoning and salad dressing mix

Vegetable oil for frying

4 to 6 (12-inch) flour tortillas, warmed

6 ounces cheddar or American cheese, grated

1/4 bottled jalapeño slices, diced (optional)

2 cups chopped cabbage tossed with 1 cup pico de gallo (optional)

Bring chicken broth to a boil in a saucepan over high heat. Slowly whisk in grits. Reduce heat to low and simmer, whisking often about 20 minutes. Stir in milk and pepper jack cheese. Season with salt and pepper, set aside, and keep warm. When ready to serve, stir in bacon.*

Cut chicken into 1-inch cubes. Whisk flour and seasoning mix together in shallow pan. Toss chicken in flour mixture and coat all sides. Remove chicken and set aside to rest while heating oil, 3–5 minutes.

Pour 3 inches of oil into bottom of a deep pot or Dutch oven. Oil should not fill pot more than 1/3 of the way up sides. Heat over medium-high heat to 365 degrees or until bubbles appear when a handle of a wooden spoon is submerged in hot oil.

Divide chicken into 3 to 4 batches and fry until golden brown on all sides and cooked completely, 8–9 minutes. Remove chicken from oil and drain on paper towels.

Assemble burritos by spooning grits onto tortillas. Sprinkle cheddar cheese and jalapeños, if using, over grits and top with fried chicken and cabbage, if using. Roll burritos as desired.

* You can replace the jalapeño grits with 1 recipe of Mexican Red or Green Rice (page 10).

☀ Makes 4 to 6 burritos

BUFFALO CHICKEN

3 tablespoons butter

1 clove garlic, minced

$1/4$ cup cayenne pepper sauce

$2^1/2$ cups large chunks shredded cooked chicken

1 large avocado, diced

$1/4$ cup diced celery

$1/4$ cup grated carrot

2 tablespoons finely sliced green onion

2 tablespoons blue cheese or ranch dressing

3 cups cooked long-grain white rice or Mexican Green Rice (page 10), warmed

4 to 6 (12-inch) flour tortillas, warmed

6 ounces blue cheese, feta, or queso fresco, crumbled

Melt butter in a large skillet with garlic over medium-low heat. Add cayenne pepper sauce and bring to a simmer. Add chicken, stir gently, and cook until most of liquid has evaporated and sauce clings to chicken, about 7 minutes.

Combine avocado, celery, carrot, and green onion in medium bowl and toss with blue cheese dressing to make an avocado salsa.

Assemble burritos by spooning rice onto tortillas. Add chicken, avocado salsa, and blue cheese crumbles. Roll burritos as desired.

☀ **Makes 4 to 6 burritos**

KANSAS CITY BARBECUE

2 pounds boneless pork shoulder roast

4 to 6 cloves garlic

3 tablespoons dark brown sugar

1 tablespoon salt

$1^1/_2$ tablespoons paprika

2 teaspoons freshly ground pepper

1 teaspoon dried thyme

$1^1/_2$ teaspoons chile powder

2 teaspoons dry mustard

$1^1/_2$ teaspoons onion powder

1 cup apple cider

$^1/_2$ cup water

4 to 6 (12-inch) flour tortillas, warmed

1 cup barbecue sauce

2 cups prepared coleslaw

Make 4 to 6 small slits into fatty side of pork, about $1^1/_2$ inches deep. Insert a garlic clove into each slit. Combine brown sugar and spices in small bowl. Reserve 1 tablespoon of spice mixture and rub remainder over entire pork shoulder. Cover pork tightly with plastic wrap and refrigerate overnight.

Preheat oven to 375 degrees.

Remove plastic wrap and bring pork to room temperature in a roasting pan with fat side up. Pour apple cider and water into pan.

Roast pork for 20 minutes, then reduce temperature to 300 degrees, and roast until pork pulls apart easily with a fork, 4–6 hours.*

Transfer pork to a large bowl and pull apart with a fork. Strain juices from pan. Stir reserved spice mixture into pan juices and spoon over pork.

Assemble burritos by spooning pork onto tortillas. Drizzle with barbecue sauce and top with coleslaw. Roll burritos as desired.

* To cook in a slow cooker, sear pork on all sides, place in cooker with apple cider and water, and cook on low for 6–8 hours or until it easily pulls apart.

☼ **Makes 4 to 6 burritos**

WEST TEXAS BEEF BARBACOA

1/2 pound bacon, diced

3 to 3 1/2 pounds boneless beef chuck roast, cut in half, visible fat removed

Salt and freshly ground pepper, to taste

1 yellow onion, chopped

2 ancho chiles, stemmed and seeded, chopped

2 tablespoons minced garlic

2 cups low-sodium vegetable broth, divided

1 cup Dr. Pepper (not diet)

1 cup barbecue sauce

2 tablespoons New Mexico chile powder

1 medium white onion, diced

1/2 cup minced fresh cilantro

4 to 6 (12-inch) flour tortillas, warmed

Salsa verde or salsa

Place bacon in a large, cold skillet. Cook over medium heat to render fat. Cook until crispy. Remove bacon from pan with a slotted spoon and set aside.

Season both sides of beef with salt and pepper and sear in bacon fat over medium-high heat until brown, about 10 minutes. Place beef in a preheated slow cooker.

Add yellow onion, anchos, and garlic to skillet and cook until onion is soft and beginning to brown, about 3 minutes. Deglaze pan with 1/2 cup of broth and pour onion mixture over beef.

Stir remaining broth, Dr. Pepper, barbecue sauce, and chile powder together in a medium bowl, and pour over beef.

Place lid on slow cooker and cook on low heat until beef is tender and pulls apart with a fork, 7–8 hours. Check often and add water, if necessary.

When ready to serve, toss bacon with white onion and cilantro in a small bowl.

Assemble burritos by spooning beef mixture onto tortillas. Add bacon-onion-cilantro mixture. Roll burritos as desired. Serve with salsa verde or salsa.

☼ **Makes 4 to 6 burritos**

ARIZONA TAMALE PIE

1 tablespoon vegetable oil

16 ounces lean ground beef

8 ounces ground pork

1 tablespoon smoked paprika

2 teaspoons ground cumin

$\frac{1}{2}$ onion, diced

3 cloves garlic, minced

1 (15-ounce) can diced tomatoes

1 (6-ounce) can tomato paste

2 tablespoons cayenne pepper sauce

1 cup fresh or frozen corn

$\frac{1}{2}$ cup sliced black olives

Salt and freshly ground pepper, to taste

3 cups low-sodium chicken broth

1 cup coarse cornmeal

3 tablespoons butter

4 to 6 (12-inch) flour tortillas, warmed

2 ounces Monterey Jack cheese, grated

Warm oil in a large skillet over medium-high heat. Add beef, pork, paprika, and cumin. Cook, breaking up meat into small pieces, until lightly browned, 3–5 minutes. Add onion and garlic and cook, another 2 minutes.

Stir into skillet tomatoes, tomato paste, and cayenne pepper sauce. Reduce heat to low and simmer until most of liquid has evaporated, about 20 minutes. Add corn and olives and cook another 5 minutes. Add salt and pepper.

Meanwhile, bring broth to a boil in a large saucepan over high heat. Slowly whisk in cornmeal. Reduce heat to low and simmer, stirring frequently, about 20 minutes. Stir in butter. Add salt and pepper.

Assemble burritos by spooning about $\frac{1}{4}$ cup of cornmeal mixture on tortillas. Add skillet mixture and sprinkle on cheese. Roll burritos as desired.

Try topping this burrito with Tomatillo Cream Sauce (page 124) for a fresh tart touch.

☀ **Makes 4 to 6 burritos**

CALIFORNIA CIOPPINO

4 ounces Italian sausage, casing removed

$^1/_2$ cup chopped yellow onion

$^1/_4$ cup each chopped celery and carrot

2 cloves garlic, minced

2 sprigs fresh thyme

1 teaspoon dried fennel seeds

1 bay leaf

$^3/_4$ cup red wine

1 (15-ounce) can diced tomatoes, with liquid

$^1/_4$ teaspoon crushed red pepper

2$^1/_2$ cups low-sodium chicken broth

1 teaspoon salt, plus more

$^1/_2$ teaspoon freshly ground pepper, plus more

4 ounces cooked crab meat, cut into $^1/_2$-inch cubes

12 medium uncooked shrimp, peeled and deveined

8 small uncooked scallops, diced

$^1/_2$ cup chopped fresh parsley, divided

2 cups cooked long-grain white rice, warmed

4 to 6 (12-inch) flour tortillas, warmed

Brown sausage in a Dutch oven or large pot over medium heat, breaking into fine pieces, about 10 minutes.

Process onion, celery, carrot, and garlic in bowl of a food processor and pulse until very small pieces. Add onion mixture to sausage and cook until softened, about 5 minutes. Add thyme, fennel, and bay leaf and cook, 2–3 minutes. Drain off extra fat.

Pour wine into pot and cook, 1–2 minutes. Add tomatoes, crushed red pepper, and broth. Season with 1 teaspoon salt and $^1/_2$ teaspoon pepper. Cover, reduce heat to low, and let simmer, about 20 minutes.

Add crab, shrimp, scallops, and $^1/_4$ cup parsley and turn off heat. Cover and let sit until seafood is cooked, about 10 minutes. Remove bay leaf. Season with salt and pepper.

Assemble burritos by spooning rice onto tortillas. Using a slotted spoon, add seafood mixture and desired amount of sauce. Sprinkle with remaining parsley. Roll burritos as desired.

☼ **Makes 4 to 6 burritos**

HAWAIIAN KALUA PORK

3 pounds boneless pork shoulder

1 1/2 tablespoons salt

1 1/2 tablespoons liquid smoke

1 fresh ripe pineapple, peeled and cored

1 tablespoon sugar (optional)

1 red bell pepper, seeded and minced

1 jalapeño, minced

1/4 small red onion, minced

1 handful fresh cilantro leaves, minced

1 cup barbecue sauce

1 habañero, stemmed and seeded, chopped

1 Napa cabbage, shredded

4 to 6 (12-inch) flour tortillas, warmed

1/2 cup cotija cheese (optional)

Cut excess fat from pork, rub with salt and liquid smoke and place in a slow cooker. Pierce pork with a carving fork every 2 inches or so. Cover and cook on low until it shreds easily with a fork, 8–10 hours.

Prepare salsa by slicing pineapple into rings or long planks. Cook on an outdoor grill or grill pan over medium-high heat until grill marks appear, 6–10 minutes. Sprinkle with sugar, if using, if pineapple is tart. Dice pineapple and reserve 1/2 cup for sauce. Toss remaining pineapple, bell pepper, jalapeño, red onion, and cilantro in medium bowl. Refrigerate until serving.

Combine barbecue sauce, reserved pineapple, and habañero in a food processor. Pulse until well blended and smooth. Heat in a small saucepan over medium heat and set aside.

Assemble burritos by spooning about 2 tablespoons of barbecue sauce on tortillas. Add pork, cabbage, and pineapple salsa. Sprinkle with cheese, if using. Roll burritos as desired.

☀ **Makes 4 to 6 burritos**

HAWAIIAN SHRIMP SHACK

1 pound (26 to 30 per pound) uncooked shrimp, peeled and deveined

2 cups cold water

1 tablespoon salt

3 tablespoons butter

3 cloves garlic, minced

2 tablespoons all-purpose flour

1 (8-ounce) can pineapple tidbits in juice

3 tablespoons dry white wine

Juice of 1 lemon (about 2 tablespoons)

1 teaspoon cayenne pepper sauce

1 tablespoon minced parsley, plus more for garnish

1 teaspoon salt

2 cups cooked long-grain white rice, warmed

4 to 6 (12-inch) flour tortillas, warmed

2 ounces Monterey Jack cheese, grated

Place shrimp on a cutting board and with a knife parallel to board, slice shrimp in half to make 2 spiral flat planks of shrimp. Place in a small bowl with water and 1 tablespoon salt. Let sit for 10 minutes. Remove from brine, rinse, and pat dry with paper towels.

Melt butter in a large skillet over medium-high heat. Add shrimp and cook until pink and cooked through, about 1 minute on each side. Transfer to a plate.

Add garlic to skillet and cook until fragrant, about 1 minute. Stir in flour and cook for 1 minute. Add juice from pineapple, wine, lemon juice, and cayenne pepper sauce, and cook, stirring constantly, until thickened, about 5 minutes. Add water, if necessary, to create a gravy consistency. Turn off heat. Stir in pineapple tidbits, parsley, and 1 teaspoon salt. Add shrimp back into skillet and toss to combine.

Assemble burritos by spooning rice and shrimp mixture onto tortillas. Sprinkle with cheese. Roll burritos as desired.

Any of the sauces in this cookbook would pair well with this burrito, with a sprinkle of cheese on top.

☀ **Makes 4 to 6 burritos**

SOUTHWEST SURF AND TURF

1¹/₂ pounds skirt or flank steak

Zest and juice of 1 lime, divided

1 red onion, diced, divided

3 cloves garlic, minced

1 tablespoon smoked paprika or chipotle chile powder

2 teaspoons ground cumin

1 tablespoon soy sauce

4 tablespoons vegetable oil, divided

1 red bell pepper, poblano, or Anaheim chile, seeded and diced

1 cup salsa

2 cups cooked long-grain white rice

¹/₂ pound uncooked shrimp, peeled and deveined

1 teaspoon salt

1¹/₄ cup refried beans, warmed

4 to 6 large flour tortillas (12-inch), warmed

2 ounces Monterey Jack cheese, grated

Place steak into a large ziplock bag. Add lime zest and ¹/₂ lime juice to a small bowl. Whisk in ¹/₂ red onion, garlic, smoked paprika, cumin, soy sauce, and 2 tablespoons oil. Add mixture to steak and squeeze with hands to evenly distribute mixture. Let sit on countertop, turning occasionally, about 1 hour, or refrigerate, 4–6 hours.

Add remaining oil to a large skillet over medium-high heat. Add remaining onion and pepper and cook until softened and lightly browned, about 5 minutes. Purée the salsa in a blender and then stir into skillet mixture. Stir in rice and heat thoroughly, about 7 minutes. Keep warm.

Let steak come to room temperature. Remove steak from bag and scrape off most of marinade. Heat an outdoor grill or broiler and cook until steak is medium rare, about 10 minutes. Transfer to plate and let sit for 10 minutes. Slice into ¹/₄-inch-thick slices across grain and squeeze remaining ¹/₂ lime juice over slices.

Season shrimp with salt. Grill or broil until pink and cooked through, about 5 minutes. Roughly chop the shrimp.

Assemble burritos by spooning beans onto tortillas. Add rice, steak. and shrimp. Sprinkle with cheese. Roll burritos as desired.

☀ **Makes 4 to 6 burritos**

LOW-COUNTRY SHRIMP AND GRITS

2 cups fresh or frozen corn kernels

1 cup whole milk

1 1/2 cups low-sodium chicken broth

3/4 cup yellow coarse grits

4 tablespoons butter, divided

1/2 pound thick-cut bacon, diced

1/2 medium white onion, minced

1 tablespoon chopped fresh thyme

1 1/2 pounds uncooked shrimp, peeled and deveined

Salt and freshly ground pepper, to taste

3 cloves garlic, minced

1/2 cup dry white wine

1/2 teaspoon cayenne pepper sauce

4 to 6 (12-inch) flour tortillas, warmed

2 green onions, green parts only, thinly sliced

1/3 cup queso fresco, crumbled

Process corn kernels in a food processor and pulse a few times until kernels are in small pieces.

Add milk and broth to a large saucepan over high heat and bring to a boil. Reduce heat to low and slowly whisk in grits. Cook until tender, whisking often, about 25 minutes. Stir in 3 tablespoons butter and corn. Season with salt and pepper. Keep warm.

Add bacon to a large skillet over medium-high heat and cook until crispy. Remove bacon pieces from pan and drain on paper towels. Pour off bacon fat, leaving about 3 tablespoons in the skillet. Add onion and thyme and cook until soft.

Season shrimp with salt and pepper. Add shrimp and garlic to skillet and cook until shrimp is pink and almost cooked through, about 3 minutes. Add wine and stir until almost evaporated, about 3 minutes. Remove pan from heat and stir in remaining butter, cayenne pepper sauce, and bacon.

Assemble burritos by spooning grits onto tortillas. Top with shrimp mixture and drizzle with pan sauce. Add green onions and queso fresco. Roll as desired.

☀ **Makes 4 to 6 burritos**

THANKSGIVING BOUNTY

2 tablespoons vegetable oil

$^1/_2$ white onion, diced

1 Anaheim chile, stemmed and seeded, diced

4 cups shredded cooked turkey

Salt and freshly ground pepper, to taste

2 cups cooked stuffing

1 (4-ounce) can chipotle chiles in adobo sauce

1 cup cranberry sauce

4 to 6 (12-inch) flour tortillas, warmed

4 ounces Monterey Jack cheese, grated

Heat oil in a large skillet over medium-high heat. Add onion and cook until translucent, 2–3 minutes. Then add Anaheim and cook until softened, 1–2 minutes. Add turkey to skillet, season with salt and pepper, and cook until heated through, about 5 minutes.

Heat the stuffing in a microwave oven until warmed through.

Mince 1 or 2 chipotle chiles and add to a small saucepan over medium heat. Reserve remaining chipotles for another use. Stir in cranberry sauce and cook until heated through, about 5 minutes.

Assemble burritos by spooning cranberry mixture on tortillas. Add turkey mixture, stuffing, and cheese. Roll burritos as desired.

For a Thanksgiving treat, try whirling a little cranberry sauce with some cream in the blender and topping this burrito.

☼ **Makes 4 to 6 burritos**

CHRISTMAS CELEBRATION

2 tablespoons vegetable oil

1 red bell pepper, seeded and cut into ¼-inch strips

1 green bell pepper, seeded and cut into ¼-inch strips

1 medium yellow onion, cut into ¼-inch strips

2 (15-ounce) cans cannellini beans, rinsed and drained

4 to 6 (12-inch) flour tortillas, warmed

1 pound deli roast beef, sliced in ¼-inch slices, warmed

2 ounces cheddar cheese, grated

2 cups Red Enchilada Sauce (page 124), warmed

2 cups Green Enchilada Sauce (page 125), warmed

Warm oil in a large skillet over medium-high heat. Cook peppers and onion until softened and lightly browned, about 5 minutes.

Mash beans with a potato masher or fork, until chunky. Add to saucepan over medium heat and cook until warmed through. Keep warm.

Assemble burritos by spooning beans onto tortillas. Add pepper-onion mixture and roast beef. Sprinkle on cheese. Roll burritos as desired. Pour Red Enchilada Sauce over half of burrito and Green Enchilada Sauce over other half of burrito.

☀ **Makes 4 to 6 burritos**

NEW MEXICO FRITO PIE

1 pound ground beef

2 cloves garlic, minced

1/2 teaspoon salt

1 teaspoon cumin

1/2 teaspoon dried Mexican oregano

2 tablespoons chile powder

1 (8-ounce) can tomato sauce

3/4 cup canned diced tomatoes with chiles

1 (15-ounce) can Ranch Style Beans or pinto beans, with liquid

2 tablespoons masa or cornmeal

1/4 cup warm water

4 to 6 (12-inch) flour tortillas, warmed

6 ounces cheddar cheese, grated

1/2 large yellow onion, finely chopped or 3 green onions, thinly sliced

3 ounces Fritos Original Corn Chips, broken

Cook beef in a large skillet, breaking into small bits, over medium-high heat until browned, about 5 minutes. Spoon off excess fat. Stir in garlic, salt, and spices. Add in tomato sauce and diced tomatoes with chiles over high heat and bring to a boil. Reduce heat to low, cover and simmer for 20 minutes. Add beans, cover, and simmer, about 15 minutes, until most of liquid has evaporated.

Stir masa and water into a small bowl. Stir into beef mixture during last 10 minutes of cooking time.

Assemble burritos by spooning beef mixture onto tortillas. Top with cheese, onion, and Fritos. Roll burritos as desired.

This recipe works well when served, or transported, as a Burrito Jar (page 5).

☀ **Makes 4 to 6 burritos**

AROUND
THE GLOBE

MASSAMAN CHICKEN CURRY (Thailand)

1 pound frozen chicken breasts

1/4 cup Massaman or red curry paste

3 tablespoons vegetable oil

1 (14-ounce) can coconut milk

1 tablespoon grated fresh ginger

2 tablespoons light brown sugar

2 tablespoons fish sauce

1 tablespoon fresh lime juice

1/4 cup peanut butter

1 tablespoon cayenne pepper sauce

1/2 onion, thinly sliced

2 large carrots, cut into 1/4-inch slices

1 large russet potato, peeled and cut in 1/2-inch cubes

2 cups cooked long-grain white rice, warmed

4 to 6 (12-inch) flour tortillas, warmed

Let chicken sit at room temperature until partially thawed, about 20 minutes.

Meanwhile, in a large skillet over medium-high heat, cook curry paste in oil, stirring constantly, for 2 minutes. Reduce heat to low and add coconut milk, ginger, brown sugar, fish sauce, lime juice, peanut butter, cayenne pepper sauce, onion, carrots, and potato and cook, covered, stirring frequently until liquid becomes very thick, about 20 minutes.

Slice chicken into 1/8-inch-thick slices. Add to skillet and cook until vegetables are fork tender, chicken is cooked through, and most of liquid has evaporated, 3–5 minutes.

Assemble burritos by spooning rice onto tortillas. Add chicken-vegetable mixture. Roll burritos as desired.

☀ **Makes 4 to 6 burritos**

RIB-EYE BAHN MI (Vietnam)

2 pounds boneless frozen rib-eye or sirloin beef

3 cloves garlic, minced

1 medium shallot, minced

3 tablespoons light brown sugar

1/2 cup fish sauce

1 large carrot, cut into 3-inch matchsticks

1 medium daikon radish, peeled and cut into 3-inch matchsticks

3 tablespoons sugar

2/3 cup rice vinegar

1 tablespoon cayenne pepper sauce

2 tablespoons vegetable oil

2 cups cooked long-grain white rice or Mexican Green Rice (page 10), warmed

4 to 6 (12-inch) flour tortillas, warmed

1 cucumber, cut into 3-inch matchsticks

1 cup chopped fresh cilantro

2 jalapeños, stemmed and seeded, minced

Let beef sit at room temperature until partially thawed, about 30 minutes. Remove all visible fat. Cut across grain into 1/8-inch-thick slices. Place beef in a ziplock bag. Add garlic, shallot, brown sugar, and fish sauce to beef and squeeze with hands to evenly distribute mixture. Let sit on countertop, turning occasionally, about 1 hour, or refrigerate, 4–6 hours.

Add carrot, daikon, sugar, vinegar, and cayenne pepper sauce to a medium bowl. Let sit at least 20 minutes. Drain but do not rinse.

Warm oil in a large skillet or grill pan over medium-high heat. Remove beef from marinade, transfer to a plate, and pat dry with paper towels. Add beef to pan in a single layer, cooking in batches as needed. Cook until browned on each side, about 5 minutes. Remove beef from skillet and let rest, about 5 minutes.

Assemble burritos by spooning rice onto tortillas. Add carrot-daikon mixture, cucumber, and cilantro. Add beef and sprinkle with jalapeño. Roll burritos as desired.

☀ **Makes 4 to 6 burritos**

BEEF BULGOGI WITH KIMCHI (Korea)

2 pounds boneless frozen rib-eye or sirloin beef

1/3 cup soy sauce

2 tablespoons brown sugar

3 tablespoons mirin

3 cloves garlic, chopped

2 tablespoons sesame oil, divided

1 Bartlett or Asian pear, peeled and cored

3 green onions, white and green parts, thinly sliced

4 to 6 (12-inch) flour tortillas, warmed

2 cups cooked long-grain white rice, warmed

4 ounces Monterey Jack cheese, grated

1 cup kimchi, most of liquid drained (optional)

4 to 6 sunny-side up cooked eggs (optional)

Let beef sit at room temperature until partially thawed, about 30 minutes. Remove all visible fat. Cut across grain into 1/8-inch-thick slices. Place beef in a ziplock bag.

In a blender, process soy sauce, brown sugar, mirin, garlic, 1 tablespoon sesame oil, and pear until smooth purée. Add to beef and squeeze with hands to evenly distribute mixture. Let sit on countertop, turning occasionally, about 1 hour, or refrigerate, 4–6 hours.

Remove beef from bag, remove excess marinade, and transfer to a plate. Drizzle beef with remaining sesame oil. Heat an outdoor grill or grill pan over medium-high heat. Add beef in a single layer, cooking in batches as needed. Cook until browned on each side, about 5 minutes. Remove beef from skillet and let rest, about 5 minutes.

Meanwhile, pour marinade from bag into a small saucepan over high heat. Bring to a boil, reduce heat to low, and simmer until reduced by half, about 5 minutes. Brush sauce on beef.

Assemble burritos by spooning beef onto tortillas. Add rice, cheese, kimchi, if using, and egg, if using. Roll burritos as desired.

This recipe works well when served as a Burrito Bowl (page 5).

☀ **Makes 4 to 6 burritos**

SUSHI

(Japan)

2 cups short-grain white rice

3 cups water

3 tablespoons rice vinegar

4 teaspoons sugar

1^1/$_2$ teaspoons salt

^{1}/$_2$ cucumber

1 red bell pepper, halved and seeded

1 ripe avocado

1 teaspoon lemon juice

4 to 6 (12-inch) flour tortillas, warmed

16 ounces cooked lump crab meat, chilled

A few sheets of nori, cut in thin strips (optional)

In large bowl, wash rice in several changes of cold water until water runs clear.

In medium saucepan over medium-high heat, combine rice and water. Cover and bring to boil. Reduce heat to low and simmer until water is absorbed, about 20 minutes. Let rice stand covered for about 10 minutes.

While rice is cooking, in small saucepan over medium heat, combine vinegar, sugar, and salt. Bring to simmer, stirring until sugar and salt dissolve. Remove from heat and cool to room temperature.

Spread warm rice on a baking sheet. Cool by fanning and stirring until steam stops rising from surface. Gradually drizzle vinegar mixture over rice, continuing to fan and stir until liquid is absorbed and rice is cooled to room temperature.

Cut all vegetables into thin 3-inch julienne pieces. Sprinkle avocado pieces with lemon juice.

Assemble burritos by spooning rice onto tortillas and then spoon on crab. Sprinkle on nori, if using. Lay a few pieces of each vegetable lengthwise on top of crab. Roll burritos as desired.

Slice burritos into thirds and wrap each piece with nori to look like sushi as a fun way to serve.

☀ **Makes 4 to 6 burritos**

CHICKEN YAKITORI

(Japan)

2 pounds boneless, skinless chicken thighs

¼ cup soy sauce

3 tablespoons mirin

3 tablespoons brown sugar

2 tablespoons grated fresh ginger

3 cloves garlic, minced

1 teaspoon cayenne pepper sauce

4 tablespoons vegetable oil, divided

4 ounces shiitake mushroom caps, thinly sliced

6 green onions, white and green parts, thinly sliced

1 cup cooked long-grain white rice, warmed

1¼ cup refried beans, warmed

4 to 6 (12-inch) flour tortillas, warmed

4 ounces Monterey Jack cheese, grated

1 lime, cut into wedges

Cut chicken into ½-inch-wide strips and place in a ziplock bag. Add soy sauce, mirin, brown sugar, ginger, garlic, and cayenne pepper sauce and squeeze with hands to evenly distribute mixture. Refrigerate, turning occasionally, 4–24 hours.

Remove chicken from bag, remove excess marinade, transfer to a plate, and pat dry with paper towels. Let chicken come to room temperature before cooking.

Warm 2 tablespoons oil in a large skillet over medium-high heat. Add mushrooms and green onions and cook until softened, about 7 minutes. Transfer vegetables to a plate.

Add remaining oil and add chicken in a single layer, cooking in batches as needed. Cook until browned on each side, about 5 minutes. Remove chicken from skillet and let rest, about 5 minutes.

Add marinade from bag, increase heat to high and bring to a boil. Reduce heat to low and simmer until reduced in half, scraping up bits from the bottom of the skillet as sauce cooks. Remove from heat and stir vegetables and chicken back into skillet.

Assemble burritos by spreading beans onto tortillas. Add rice and chicken mixture. Sprinkle with cheese and drizzle with lime juice. Roll burritos as desired.

☀ **Makes 4 to 6 burritos**

CASHEW CHICKEN

(China)

3 boneless, skinless chicken breasts

1/2 pound fresh or frozen snow peas

1/2 pound button or cremini mushrooms

1 rib celery

1 (8-ounce) can water chestnuts, drained and sliced

4 green onions, divided

1/4 cup soy sauce, plus more for garnish

2 tablespoons cornstarch

2 teaspoons sugar

4 tablespoons vegetable oil, divided

4 ounces raw, unsalted cashews

1 cup low-sodium chicken broth

2 cups cooked long-grain white rice

4 to 6 (12-inch) flour tortillas, warmed

1 teaspoon sesame oil (optional)

Slice chicken into 1-inch cubes. Remove ends and strings from snow peas. Slice mushrooms, celery, water chestnuts, and white part of onions into 1/4-inch slices. Slice green part of onions into 1-inch lengths. Set aside.

Mix soy sauce, cornstarch, and sugar in a small bowl.

Heat 1 tablespoon oil in a large skillet or wok over medium-high heat. Add cashews and cook, shaking pan until lightly toasted, about 2 minutes. Remove cashews from pan, set aside. Add 1 1/2 tablespoons oil to pan and cook chicken until it turns opaque. Transfer to a plate. Add remaining oil to pan over medium-high heat, add snow peas, mushrooms, celery, and white part of green onions and cook until celery is tender and begins to brown, about 5 minutes.

Pour in broth and bring to boil. Stir soy sauce mixture into skillet and cook until sauce is thickened, stirring constantly. Add chicken, cover, and simmer until chicken is cooked through, about 2 minutes. Add green part of onions into chicken. Sprinkle with cashews.

Assemble burritos by spooning rice onto tortillas. Add chicken mixture and sprinkle with soy sauce and sesame oil, if using. Roll burritos as desired.

☀ **Makes 4 to 6 burritos**

MONGOLIAN BEEF

2 pounds flank steak

$1/4$ cup vegetable oil, divided

1 tablespoon toasted sesame oil

$1/2$ cup soy sauce

$1/2$ cup Shaoxing wine or dry sherry

2 tablespoons minced garlic, divided

1 cup thinly sliced green onions, white and green parts, divided

$1/2$ tablespoon freshly ground pepper

1 tablespoon minced fresh ginger

2 tablespoons brown sugar

1 cup fermented or regular black beans, rinsed and drained

2 cups cooked long-grain white rice, warmed

4 to 6 (12-inch) flour tortillas, warmed

Cut flank steak lengthwise into $1^1/2$-inch-wide strips. Cut each strip across grain into slices that are $1/4$ inch thick.

Mix 2 tablespoons vegetable oil, sesame oil, soy sauce, wine, 1 tablespoon garlic, $1/2$ cup green onions, and black pepper in a large ziplock bag. Add beef and squeeze with hands to evenly distribute mixture.. Refrigerate 6-8 hours.

Remove beef from marinade, transfer to a plate, and pat dry with paper towels. Reserve marinade.

Heat remaining oil in a wok or large skillet over high heat. Add ginger, remaining garlic, and 1 tablespoon green onions and cook until tender, 1-2 minutes. Add beef to wok and cook until medium-rare, 4-5 minutes. Remove beef from wok, set aside, and keep warm. Stir brown sugar into reserved marinade and pour into wok and bring to a boil. Reduce heat to medium-low and simmer to thicken marinade, about 5 minutes.

Assemble burritos by combining beans and rice then spooning onto tortillas. Top with beef and sprinkle with remaining green onions. Drizzle with sauce. Roll burritos as desired.

☀ **Makes 4 to 6 burritos**

HULI HULI CHICKEN

1¹/₄ cups soy sauce, divided

1 cup water

4 tablespoons vegetable oil, divided

4 tablespoons minced garlic, divided

4 tablespoons grated fresh ginger, divided

4 boneless, skinless chicken breasts

1¹/₂ cups pineapple juice

¹/₄ cup brown sugar

¹/₄ cup ketchup

¹/₄ cup rice vinegar

1 tablespoon cayenne pepper sauce

1 cup pineapple tidbits

¹/₄ cup chopped fresh cilantro

4 cups cooked long-grain white rice, warmed

4 to 6 (12-inch) flour tortillas, warmed

2 ounces Monterey Jack cheese, grated

Stir 1 cup soy sauce, water, 2 tablespoons oil, 3 tablespoons garlic, and 3 tablespoons ginger in medium bowl. Pour into a ziplock bag.

Pound chicken to uniform thickness, about ¹/₂ inch thick. Add chicken to bag. Let sit on countertop, turning occasionally, 1 hour, or refrigerate up to 4 hours.

Combine remaining soy sauce, pineapple juice, brown sugar, ketchup, vinegar, and cayenne pepper sauce in medium saucepan over high heat. Add remaining garlic and ginger. Simmer until thickened, whisking frequently.

Heat an outdoor grill or broiler.

Remove chicken from marinade and pat dry. Discard marinade. Brush chicken with remaining oil. Grill over medium heat until cooked through, about 18 minutes. The last few minutes of cooking time, brush sauce on both sides of chicken, repeating until coated in a thick layer of sauce. Let chicken cool to warm and then slice across the grain into thin slices.

Stir remaining sauce, pineapple tidbits, and cilantro into rice.

Assemble burritos by spooning chicken onto tortillas. Add rice mixture and sprinkle on cheese. Roll burritos as desired.

☀ **Makes 4 to 6 burritos**

LEMON CHICKEN AND YAM (Peru)

2 tablespoons vegetable oil, divided

1 tablespoon smoked paprika

1 tablespoon ground cumin

2 teaspoons salt, divided

1 teaspoon cayenne pepper sauce

1 teaspoon dried oregano leaves

3 cloves garlic, chopped

Zest and juice of 1 lemon

4 chicken thighs

1 (16-ounce) yam, peeled and cut into $1/2$-inch cubes

1 bell pepper, any color, seeded and diced

1 sweet white onion, diced

4 to 6 (12-inch) flour tortillas, warmed

2 ounces Monterey Jack cheese, grated

Preheat oven to 400 degrees.

Stir together 1 tablespoon oil, paprika, cumin, 1 teaspoon salt, cayenne pepper sauce, oregano, garlic, lemon zest, and juice in small bowl. Slice the emptied lemon halves into $1/4$-inch slices and set aside. Rub marinade on chicken, including under skin.

Brush a 9 x 13-inch pan with remaining oil. Add yam, bell pepper, and onion, coating in oil, and spread into pan. Sprinkle with remaining salt. Place chicken, skin side up, on vegetables. Place lemon slices in between chicken.

Bake for 30 minutes and remove from oven. Remove chicken pieces and stir vegetables. Place chicken back on top of vegetables, skin side up, and bake for another 20 minutes.

Remove from oven and remove and discard lemon slices. Transfer chicken to clean plate to rest, about 5 minutes. Chop into small pieces. Using a fork, mash yam slightly and then toss all vegetables and chicken together in a medium bowl.

Assemble burritos by spooning chicken mixture onto tortillas. Sprinkle on cheese. Roll burritos as desired.

☀ **Makes 4 to 6 burritos**

PICADILLO TURKEY

(Cuba)

2 tablespoons vegetable oil

1 pound ground turkey

1 tablespoon ground cumin

1 tablespoon smoked paprika

2 small red bliss potatoes, diced

1/2 medium onion, diced

6 cloves garlic, minced

1/2 cup dry white wine

1/2 red bell pepper, seeded and diced

6 pimiento-stuffed green olives, diced

1/2 cup raisins, diced

1/4 cup capers, diced

1 (8-ounce) can tomato sauce

Salt and freshly ground pepper, to taste

4 to 6 (12-inch) flour tortillas, warmed

4 ounces Monterey Jack cheese, grated

Warm oil in a large skillet over medium-high heat. Add turkey and cook, breaking turkey up into small bits, until lightly browned, about 8 minutes. Remove turkey from skillet, leaving oil.

Add cumin and paprika to skillet over medium-high heat. Add potatoes and cook until fork tender and browned, about 5 minutes. Add onion and cook until onion is translucent, about 3 minutes. Add garlic and cook until fragrant, about 1 minute. Add wine, scraping up browned bits on pan bottom, and cook until wine is reduced by half.

Add cooked turkey, bell pepper, olives, raisins, capers, and tomato sauce to skillet. Simmer and stir until all of liquid has evaporated, about 10 minutes. Add salt and pepper.

Assemble burritos by spooning turkey mixture onto tortillas. Sprinkle with cheese. Roll burritos as desired.

☀ **Makes 4 to 6 burritos**

CRISPY CITRUS BEEF

(Cuba)

2 pounds boneless chuck roast

2 teaspoons salt

3 cloves garlic, minced

1 tablespoon ground cumin

2 tablespoons orange juice concentrate

Zest and juice of 1 lime

2 tablespoons red wine vinegar

3 tablespoons vegetable oil, divided

1 sweet white onion, cut in half and then into 1/4-inch slices

Salt, to taste

1 (15-ounce) can refried beans, warmed

4 to 6 (12-inch) flour tortillas, warmed

2 ounces cheddar cheese, grated

1 cup pico de gallo

Remove visible fat from beef and cut into 2-inch chunks. Place in a slow cooker and toss with salt. Cover and cook, stirring every 2 hours, until beef cubes are fork tender, on high for 6–7 hours, or on low for 8–10 hours. Remove beef from slow cooker and let cool to room temperature.

Add garlic, cumin, orange juice concentrate, zest and juice of lime, and vinegar to a small bowl and stir.

Warm 1 tablespoon oil in a large skillet over medium-high heat. Add onion and cook until softened, 3–5 minutes. Pour orange juice mixture and slow cooker liquid into skillet, cooking until liquid is almost evaporated. Empty skillet into a bowl and then wipe skillet with a paper towel.

Smash cooled beef pieces flat by pressing them between sheets of plastic wrap with a rolling pin.

Warm 1 tablespoon oil in large skillet over medium-high heat. Add half of flattened beef pieces in a single layer. Cook until crispy and browned on both sides. Add remaining oil and repeat process for other half of flattened beef. Shred beef with a fork and stir into onion mixture in bowl, seasoning with salt.

Assemble burritos by spooning refried beans onto tortillas. Add beef mixture. Sprinkle on cheese and pico de gallo. Roll burritos as desired.

☀ **Makes 4 to 6 burritos**

CHICKEN MARRAKESH

(Morocco)

2 teaspoons mild curry powder

1 tablespoon ground cumin

1 1/2 teaspoons salt

1/2 cup olive oil, divided

3 cups peeled and diced sweet potatoes

1/3 cup whole almonds with skin, coarsely chopped

1/4 cup pepitas

1 1/2 tablespoons cumin seeds

1 large tomato, seeded and diced

4 green onions, white and green parts, thinly sliced

2 cups chopped fresh cilantro

1/4 cup red wine vinegar

1 clove garlic, minced

3 cups cooked shredded chicken meat

4 to 6 (12-inch) flour tortillas, warmed

Preheat oven to 375 degrees.

Add curry powder, cumin, salt, and 4 tablespoons oil to a small bowl and combine. Toss half of mixture with sweet potatoes. Spread on a baking sheet and roast until fork tender, 35–40 minutes.

Toss almonds and pepitas with remaining spice mixture and spread on a baking sheet. Toast until fragrant, about 8 minutes. Sprinkle cumin seeds over nuts 2 minutes before removing from oven and toast until cumin is fragrant. Remove from oven and pulse almond mixture in a food processor until nuts are in small bits.

Add tomato, green onions, and cilantro to a small bowl and combine. Set aside.

Whisk vinegar, garlic, and remaining oil in a large bowl. Stir in almond mixture. Add chicken and roasted sweet potatoes and toss.

Assemble burritos by spooning chicken-sweet potato mixture onto tortillas. Top with tomato mixture. Roll burritos as desired.

☼ **Makes 4 to 6 burritos**

LAMB KABOBS WITH TZATZIKI (Greece)

2 pounds leg of lamb, trimmed of fat and cut into 1-inch cubes

3/4 cup olive oil, divided

1/2 cup fresh lemon juice, divided

2 teaspoons lemon zest, divided

6 cloves garlic, minced, divided

1 tablespoon minced fresh rosemary

2 teaspoons ground pepper

1 tablespoon whole grain mustard

1/2 cucumber, peeled, seeded, and finely grated

1/2 cup Greek yogurt

1 tablespoon chopped fresh dill,

Salt and freshly ground pepper, to taste

2 cups cherry tomatoes

1/4 cup olive oil

1 handful fresh mint or fresh basil, chopped

4 to 6 (12-inch) flour tortillas, warmed

8 ounces feta cheese, crumbled

Place lamb in a ziplock bag. Add 1/2 cup olive oil, 1/3 cup lemon juice, 1 1/2 teaspoons lemon zest, 4 cloves garlic, rosemary, 2 teaspoons pepper, and mustard to lamb and squeeze with hands to evenly distribute mixture. Refrigerate 4 hours or up to overnight.

Press excess liquid from cucumber. Add yogurt, drained cucumber, 1 clove garlic, remaining lemon zest, 1/2 tablespoon lemon juice, dill, and salt and pepper. Set aside.

Heat oven to broil. Soak 30 bamboo skewers in water to cover for 30 minutes before using in broiler.

Toss cherry tomatoes with olive oil, remaining clove garlic, salt, and pepper in a small bowl. Broil on a baking sheet until the skins burst, about 7 minutes. Toss with mint.

Remove lamb from marinade, season with salt and pepper, and thread on bamboo skewers, leaving a small space between pieces. Broil on all sides, turning every 1–2 minutes and cook to desired doneness, 7–8 minutes. Remove lamb from broiler and let rest 5 minutes. Chop lamb into smaller pieces, if desired.

Assemble the burritos by spooning lamb onto tortillas. Add cherry tomatoes, feta cheese, and drizzle with Tzatziki sauce. Roll burritos as desired.

☀ **Makes 4 to 6 burritos**

CHICKEN TIKKA MASALA

(India)

3 tablespoons vegetable oil

1/4 teaspoon red pepper flakes

1/2 white onion, diced

3 cloves garlic, chopped

2 tablespoons grated fresh ginger

1 teaspoon ground cumin

1 tablespoon garam masala powder

1 teaspoon salt

1 (15-ounce) can tomato purée

1 tablespoon cayenne pepper sauce

1/3 cup plain yogurt

4 cups 1-inch pieces cooked chicken

1 (15-ounce) can refried beans, warmed

4 to 6 (12-inch) flour tortillas, warmed

4 ounces Monterey Jack cheese, grated

Warm oil in a large skillet over medium-high heat. Add red pepper flakes and onion and cook until onion is translucent, about 3 minutes. Stir in garlic, ginger, cumin, garam masala, and salt and cook until fragrant, about 1 minute.

Add tomato purée and cayenne pepper sauce to skillet and stir, scraping up browned bits from bottom of skillet. Reduce heat to medium-low and simmer, stirring frequently, about 5 minutes. Stir in yogurt and chicken. Remove from heat. Let sit for 5 minutes.

Assemble burritos by spooning refried beans onto tortillas. Add chicken mixture and sprinkle on cheese. Roll burritos as desired.

Spoon on diced pico de gallo for a fresh addition to this burrito.

☀ **Makes 4 to 6 burritos**

VEGGIE MULLIGATAWNY

(India)

3 tablespoons butter

2 tablespoons curry powder

1 medium yellow onion, diced

1 medium carrot, diced

$1/2$ cup sweetened coconut

4 cloves garlic, chopped

1 tablespoon grated fresh ginger

1 rib celery, diced

1 tablespoon tomato paste

1 cup low-sodium chicken broth

1 cup coconut milk

1 tablespoon fresh lime juice

2 cups cooked long-grain white rice or Mexican Green Rice (page 10), warmed

4 to 6 (12-inch) flour tortillas, warmed

$1/4$ cup minced fresh cilantro

1 (15-ounce) can lentils, drained and rinsed

2 ounces Monterey Jack cheese, grated

Melt butter in a large skillet over medium-high heat. Add curry powder, onion, and carrot and cook, stirring frequently, about 3 minutes. Add coconut, garlic, ginger, and celery and cook until all vegetables are softened, another 3–5 minutes.

Whisk tomato paste, broth, coconut milk, and lime juice in medium bowl. Stir into skillet and cook until almost all liquid has evaporated, about 7 minutes.

Assemble burritos by spooning rice onto tortillas. Add skillet mixture. Sprinkle with cilantro, lentils, and cheese. Roll burritos as desired.

☀ **Makes 4 to 6 burritos**

CORNED BEEF AND CABBAGE   (Ireland)

2 pounds corned beef brisket, cooked according to package directions*

2 tablespoons vegetable oil

1 tablespoon ground cumin

1 medium sweet white onion, cut into 3-inch matchsticks

2 jalapeños, stemmed and seeded, cut into 3-inch matchsticks

1/2 head cabbage

1 teaspoon salt

1 tablespoon red wine vinegar

1 tablespoon cayenne pepper sauce

1/4 cup chopped fresh cilantro

1 (15-ounce) can refried beans, warmed

4 to 6 (12-inch) flour tortillas, warmed

2 ounces Monterey Jack cheese, grated

Cut corned beef into 1/4-inch-thick slices, and then into 1/4-inch slices across the grain. Set aside.

Warm oil in a large skillet over medium-high heat. Add cumin and stir until fragrant, about 1 minute. Add onion and jalapeños and cook until onion and pepper are lightly browned and softened, stirring frequently, about 3 minutes.

Cut cabbage into quarters. Remove the white core and discard. Cut cabbage across the diameter into 1/4-inch-thick slices. Add cabbage and salt to skillet, cover, and cook, stirring frequently, until cabbage is softened, about 15 minutes. Add vinegar and cayenne pepper sauce. Stir and cook until liquid has evaporated, about 3 minutes. Remove from heat and stir in cilantro.

Assemble burritos by spooning beans onto tortillas. Add cabbage mixture and corned beef. Sprinkle on cheese. Roll burritos as desired.

* You may substitute 2 pounds of deli corned beef, cut into 1/4-inch-thick slices and then cut into thin strips across the grain.

☼ Makes 4 to 6 burritos

SEAFOOD PAELLA

(Spain)

1 pound uncooked shrimp, peeled and deveined

6 cloves garlic, minced, divided

1 teaspoon salt, divided

4 tablespoons olive oil, divided

2 boneless, skinless chicken thighs

1/2 pound Spanish chorizo, cut in 1/4-inch half-moon slices

1 medium sweet onion, diced

1 red bell pepper, seeded and diced

1 tablespoon ground turmeric

1/2 cup dry white wine

2 cups low-sodium chicken broth

1 cup uncooked medium-grain rice

2 bay leaves

3/4 cup frozen peas

1/4 cup chopped fresh parsley

2 tablespoons fresh lemon juice

4 to 6 (12-inch) flour tortillas, warmed

Chop shrimp and add to a small bowl. Add half of garlic, salt, and 2 tablespoons oil. Let sit for at 10 minutes.

Meanwhile, warm remaining oil in a large skillet over medium-high heat. Add chicken and cook until golden brown but still slightly pink in the center, 3–5 minutes on each side. Add shrimp mixture to skillet and cook another 3 minutes, until shrimp is cooked through. Remove chicken and shrimp from skillet. When cool, cut chicken into small pieces.

Add chorizo, onion, and bell pepper to skillet. Cook, stirring occasionally, until onion is translucent, about 5 minutes. Add turmeric and cook, 1 more minute. Add wine, scraping up browned bits on pan bottom, and cook until wine is reduced by half.

Add broth, rice, and bay leaves and bring to a boil over high heat. Reduce to low heat, cover, and cook until rice has softened and absorbed liquid, about 20 minutes. Add chicken, shrimp, peas, parsley, and lemon juice.

Assemble burritos by spooning paella mixture onto tortillas. Roll burritos as desired.

☀ **Makes 4 to 6 burritos**

ITALIAN SAUSAGE, KALE, AND CANNELLINI

(Italy)

1 tablespoon vegetable oil

1 pound spicy Italian sausage, casings removed

1 large shallot, diced

4 cups chopped kale

1/4 cup dry white wine

2 (15-ounce) cans cannellini beans, rinsed and drained

2 cups low-sodium chicken broth

4 to 6 (12-inch) flour tortillas, warmed

4 ounces mozzarella cheese, grated

Warm oil in a large skillet over medium-high heat. Add sausage and cook until lightly browned, breaking into small bits, about 10 minutes.

Add shallot and kale and cook until shallot is softened, 1–2 minutes. Add wine, scraping up browned bits on pan bottom and cook until wine is reduced by half.

Mash 1 can of beans with a potato masher or fork, until chunky. Add mashed beans, unmashed beans, and broth to skillet. Simmer until most of liquid has evaporated, about 10 minutes.

Assemble burritos by spooning sausage mixture onto tortillas. Sprinkle with cheese. Roll burritos as desired.

Red Enchilada Sauce (page 124) gives this burrito a nice finishing touch.

☀ **Makes 4 to 6 burritos**

SWEET TREATS

MINI APPLE CHIMICHANGAS

Vegetable oil for frying

2 tablespoons unsalted butter

1/2 cup light brown sugar

6 large Granny Smith apples, peeled, cored, and diced

1/2 teaspoon cinnamon plus more for dusting

1/4 teaspoon ground nutmeg

Pinch of salt

1 teaspoon fresh lemon juice

4 to 6 (10-inch) flour tortillas, warmed

1 cup heavy cream

2 to 3 tablespoons caramel sauce

Powdered sugar for dusting

Heat oil to 375 degrees in a deep fryer or large pot filled with no more than 3 inches of oil.

Melt butter in a large skillet over medium heat. Add brown sugar and stir until melted and smooth. Add apples and cook until fork tender, but not mushy, about 7 minutes. Remove from heat and sprinkle cinnamon, nutmeg, and salt over apples and stir in lemon juice.

Remove edges on three sides of tortillas to square off edges. Using a slotted spoon, spoon apple filling into center of tortillas and roll into burritos. Lay rolled burritos seam side down and let sit for a few minutes. Secure with toothpicks.

Use scraps of tortilla to test temperature of oil. Tortillas should bubble and float to top when oil is proper temperature. Fry chimichangas until golden brown and crispy. Drain on paper towels.

Pour cream into chilled glass bowl and whip halfway to soft peaks. Drizzle caramel sauce onto cream while whipping to medium peaks. Dust apple chimichangas with powdered sugar. Top with caramel whipped cream. Dust cream with cinnamon.

☀ **Makes 4 to 6 burritos**

S'MORES MINI CHIMICHANGAS

2 teaspoons toasted and diced walnuts

1/2 tablespoon unsalted butter

2 tablespoons graham cracker crumbs

Pinch of cinnamon

Pinch of salt

2 (1.55-ounce) Hershey's milk chocolate bars

4 to 6 (6-inch) flour tortillas, warmed

36 miniature marshmallows (about 1/2 cup)

Vegetable oil for frying

1/4 cup powdered sugar, for dusting

Toast walnuts in a small, dry skillet until fragrant. Add butter and remove from heat as soon as it melts. Stir in graham cracker crumbs, cinnamon, and salt.

Divide each chocolate bar into 4 sections. Place 1 section on each tortilla. Top with 6 mini marsh-mallows and 1 teaspoon graham cracker mixture. Chop remaining chocolate and sprinkle over top, if desired. Roll into burritos and secure with toothpicks.

Heat oil to 375 degrees in a deep fryer or large pot filled with no more than 3 inches of oil.

Fry chimichangas until crispy and golden brown, about 2 minutes per side. Drain on paper towels. Remove toothpicks and dust with powdered sugar.

☀ **Makes 4 to 6 burritos**

BANANAS FOSTER CHIMICHANGAS

4 tablespoons unsalted butter

1 cup brown sugar

1/2 teaspoon cinnamon

1 teaspoon fresh lemon juice

Pinch of salt

4 firm ripe bananas

1/3 cup spiced rum

4 to 6 (12-inch) flour tortillas, warmed

Vegetable oil for frying

1 teaspoon cinnamon

1/4 cup sugar

Vanilla ice cream

Melt butter in a large skillet over medium heat. Add brown sugar and stir until dissolved and thickened, 2–3 minutes. Add cinnamon, lemon juice, and salt.

Peel bananas and slice into 1/2-inch-wide slices. Add to brown sugar mixture. Stir to coat bananas in brown sugar sauce. Remove pan from heat and carefully add rum. Ignite rum with a long match or long kitchen lighter. Return pan to heat and baste bananas in sauce until they begin to soften. Continue basting until flames goes out. Remove bananas from pan and chill in refrigerator to stop them from cooking further.

Assemble burritos by spooning bananas onto tortillas. Add a spoonful of sauce. Roll into burritos. Lay burritos seam side and let sit a few minutes. Secure with toothpicks.

Heat oil to 375 degrees in a deep fryer or large pot filled with no more than 3 inches of oil.

Fry chimichangas until crispy and golden brown, about 2 minutes per side. Drain on paper towels. Remove toothpicks.

Mix cinnamon and sugar together and sprinkle both sides of chimichangas. Serve with ice cream. Spoon remaining sauce over ice cream.

☀ **Makes 4 to 6 burritos**

DULCE DE LECHE CHEESECAKE BITES

8 ounces cream cheese, room temperature

1/4 cup sour cream

4 tablespoons sugar, divided

1 teaspoon vanilla

4 to 6 (8-inch) flour tortillas, warmed

1/2 cup dulce de leche or caramel sauce, chilled

Vegetable oil for frying

2 teaspoons cinnamon

With a stand mixer and paddle attachment, beat cream cheese, sour cream, 1 tablespoon sugar, and vanilla until fluffy. Chill mixture in refrigerator until firm and can be sliced, 1-2 hours. Slice mixture into rectangles 3 1/2 inches long, 1 1/2 inches wide, and 1 inch thick. Freeze rectangles until hardened, about 2 hours.

Assemble burritos by placing cream cheese rectangles on tortillas. Top with spoonfuls of dulce de leche. Roll into burritos and secure with toothpicks.

Heat oil to 375 degrees in a deep fryer or large pot filled with no more than 3 inches of oil.

Deep fry cheesecake bites until golden brown and crispy, but not hard. Drain on paper towels and remove toothpicks.

Mix remaining 3 tablespoons sugar and cinnamon together and sprinkle on all sides of cheesecake bites. Serve warm so filling is still soft and creamy.

Note: This recipe is great using pre-made cheesecake cut into rectangles.

☀ **Makes 4 to 6 burritos**

MANGO COCONUT STICKY RICE

2 1/4 cups glutinous rice

1 teaspoon vanilla extract

1 large banana leaf (found at Latin or Asian markets), optional

1/2 cup unsweetened coconut milk

2 large ripe mangos, peeled and diced

4 tablespoons sugar, divided

1 tablespoon fresh lime juice

1 teaspoon lime zest

1/2 teaspoon cayenne pepper

1/3 cup caramel sauce

4 to 6 (8-inch) flour tortillas, warmed

Vegetable oil for frying or brushing on burritos

2 teaspoons ground cinnamon

The day before, rinse extra starch from rice. Repeat until water runs clear. Pour in enough water to cover rice and add vanilla. Refrigerate overnight.

Prepare a bamboo steamer by placing a square of banana leaf (with a hole cut in the center) or cheesecloth on bottom of steamer. Drain rice and distribute rice evenly over banana leaf or cheesecloth. Steam rice until fully cooked but not mushy, about 45 minutes. The rice should be sticky. Transfer rice to a large serving bowl. Add coconut milk and toss lightly.

Meanwhile, toss mangos with 1 tablespoon sugar, lime juice, lime zest, and cayenne pepper in medium bowl.

Assemble burritos by spooning coconut rice onto tortillas. Drizzle with caramel sauce, add mango, and roll into burritos.

Heat oil to 375 degrees in a deep fryer or large pot filled with no more than 3 inches or oil, or brush with oil and bake at 350 degrees until golden brown and crispy. Mix remaining sugar and cinnamon together and sprinkle over burritos.

☼ Makes 4 to 6 burritos

SAUCES

Red Chile Mole

2 dried Anaheim or ancho chiles, stemmed and seeded

2 tablespoons golden raisins

2 tablespoons sesame seeds

1¹/₂ teaspoons peppercorns

¹/₂ cinnamon stick

1¹/₂ teaspoons dried Mexican oregano

2 sprigs fresh thyme

2 tablespoons corn oil

1 onion, sliced

1 jalapeño, stemmed and seeded, sliced

2 cloves garlic, sliced

1 (15-ounce) can diced, fire-roasted tomatoes

1 ounce Mexican chocolate, chopped

2 tablespoons almond butter

1¹/₂ cups low-sodium chicken broth

1 teaspoon salt

Tear dried chiles into pieces and toast in a dry skillet over medium-high heat until fragrant and color changes, about 3 minutes. Put chiles in a bowl with raisins and pour in enough boiling water to cover. Set aside for 30 minutes.

Using same skillet over medium-high heat, toast sesame seeds, peppercorns, cinnamon stick, oregano, and thyme for 2 minutes. Grind into a fine powder in a spice grinder. Place powder in a blender.

Warm oil in skillet over medium-high heat. Add onion and jalapeño and cook until onion softens, about 5 minutes. Add garlic and cook until fragrant, about 1 minute.

Put onion mixture, tomatoes with juice, chocolate, and almond butter in blender with spices. Drain chiles (reserving the liquid) and add to blender. Add broth to blender and purée. Check for desired thickness. Add some of reserved chile liquid if mole is too thick. Season with salt.

☀ **Makes 5 cups**

Red Enchilada Sauce

1/4 cup vegetable oil

2 tablespoons all-purpose flour

1/2 cup finely diced onion

1/2 cup New Mexico red chile powder

1 teaspoon garlic powder

1/2 teaspoon ground cumin

1 teaspoon dried Mexican oregano

2 1/2 cups low-sodium beef, chicken, or vegetable broth

1 teaspoon salt

1/4 teaspoon freshly ground pepper

Warm oil in a medium saucepan over medium-high heat. Add flour and stir until mixture begins to bubble, about 2 minutes. Add onion and cook until softened and beginning to brown, about 5 minutes. Stir in chile powder, garlic powder, cumin, and oregano and cook until fragrant, about 1 minute. Slowly add broth while whisking to remove any lumps. Bring to a boil. Reduce heat to low and simmer for 10–15 minutes. Season with salt and pepper.

 Makes 4 cups

Tomatillo Cream Sauce

1 1/2 pounds tomatillos

2 tablespoons light olive oil

3 tablespoons minced shallot

3 cups heavy cream

1/2 cup sour cream

1 teaspoon salt

1/2 teaspoon white pepper

Preheat oven to 450 degrees.

Roast tomatillos on a baking sheet until skins are lightly browned. Remove from oven and cool. Remove skins and purée in a blender.

Warm oil in a small skillet over medium-high heat. Add shallot and cook until translucent, about 2 minutes. Add cream and sour cream. Simmer until slightly thickened. Add tomatillo purée. Season with salt and white pepper.

Makes 5 cups

Green Enchilada Sauce

2 pounds tomatillos, husks removed

1 sweet white onion

1 poblano chile, stemmed and seeded

2 jalapeños, stemmed and seeded

2 tablespoons vegetable oil

6 cloves garlic

1 tablespoon ground cumin

1 cup fresh cilantro leaves

2 teaspoons salt

1 tablespoon cayenne pepper sauce

Preheat oven to 450 degrees.

Cut tomatillos in half. Cut onion into quarters. Cut chiles into strips. Toss tomatillos, onion, poblano, and jalapeño in oil in medium bowl. Spread on a baking sheet in a single layer and bake until softened and lightly browned, about 20 minutes. Add garlic and bake another 10 minutes. Remove from oven and add vegetables to a blender.

Add cumin, cilantro, salt, and cayenne pepper sauce to blender and process until smooth. Taste and add additional salt and cayenne pepper sauce as desired.

☀ **Makes 4 cups**

Chimichurri Sauce

1/2 cup minced fresh parsley or cilantro

2 tablespoons minced shallot

3 tablespoons red wine vinegar

3 tablespoons olive oil

1/2 tablespoon minced jalapeño

1 clove garlic, minced

1/2 teaspoon salt

1/2 teaspoon freshly ground pepper

Add parsley, shallot, red wine vinegar, oil, jalapeño, garlic, salt, and pepper to a small bowl. Stir to combine, set aside, and let flavors blend before serving.

☀ **Makes 1 cup**

INDEX

almonds, 105
Anaheim chile, 122
ancho chile, 28, 70, 81
andouille sausage, 63, 64
apple, 18, 115
Arizona Tamale Pie, 73
Arroz con Pollo, 33
avocado, 10, 13, 46, 55, 56, 59, 66, 93
bacon, 6, 13, 19, 33, 65, 70, 80
Baja Seafood, 59
banana leaf, 32, 212
Bananas Foster Chimichangas, 118
bananas, 118
barbecue sauce, 50, 69, 70, 76
Beef Bulgogi with Kimchi, 91
beef, 24, 28, 40, 73, 79, 83, 84, 88, 91, 96, 103, 109
beets, 49, 70
bell pepper, 14, 33, 36, 40, 45, 56, 60, 64, 76, 79, 83, 93, 100, 102, 110
Black Bean, Corn, and Quinoa, 45
black beans, 29, 30, 35, 45, 60, 61, 96
black olives, 73
blue cheese dressing, 66
blue cheese, 66
buffalo chicken, 66
Burrito Bowls, 5
Burrito Jars, 5
Burrito Spirals, 5
Butternut Squash and Apple Hash, 18
butternut squash, 18, 52
cabbage, 65, 76, 109
Cajun Jambalaya, 64
California Cioppino, 74
California Dreamin', 13

Cancun Grilled Chicken, 44
cannellini beans, 20, 49, 83, 112
capers, 102
caramel sauce, 121
Carne Asada, 24
carrot, 66, 74, 87, 88, 108
Cashew Chicken, 95
Cauliflower Rice and Poblano, 56
cauliflower, 56
celery, 66, 74, 95, 018
cheddar cheese, 13, 14, 15, 19, 29, 30, 35, 40, 61, 65, 83, 84, 103
Chicken Marrakesh, 105
Chicken Mole, 35
Chicken Tikka Masala, 107
Chicken Tinga, 29
Chicken Yakitori, 94
chicken, 29, 33, 35, 36, 44, 50, 64, 65, 66, 94, 95, 99, 100, 105, 107, 110
Chile Verde, 23
Chimichangas, 5
Chimichurri Sauce, 43, 46, 60, 125
chipotle chile, 29, 81
chocolate, 116, 122
Chorizo and Potato, 16
chorizo, 16, 110
Christmas Celebration, 83
cilantro, 10, 20, 24, 27, 32, 39, 45, 49, 52, 70, 76, 88, 99, 105, 108, 109, 125
Coca Cola, 39
coconut milk, 87, 108, 121
coconut, 108
cotija cheese, 24, 60, 76
coleslaw, 69
corn, 45, 73, 80

Corned Beef and Cabbage, 109
cornmeal, 73
crab meat, 74, 93
cranberry, 81
cream cheese, 119
Crispy Burritos, 4
Crispy Citrus Beef, 103
cucumber, 88, 93, 106
Denver Omelet, 14
Double-Rolled Bean and Cheese, 30
Dr. Pepper, 70
Dulce de Leche Cheesecake Bites, 119
feta cheese, 106
fish sauce, 87, 88
Freezing Burritos, 5
Fritos Original Corn Chips, 84
goat cheese, 49
green chiles, 19, 40
Green Enchilada Sauce, 83, 125
green olives, 102
green salsa (salsa verde), 10, 33, 70
grits, 65, 80
guacamole, 24, 44
guajillo chile, 28
habañero, 44, 50, 76
ham, 14
Hash Browns and Eggs, 15
Hawaiian Kalua Pork, 76
Hawaiian Shrimp Shack, 77
heavy cream, 115, 124
Homemade Flour Tortillas, 9
hominy, 39
Huevos El Diablo, 20
Huli Huli Chicken, 99
Italian sausage, 74, 112

Italian Sausage, Kale, and Cannellini, 112
jalapeños, 20, 24, 43, 44, 45, 59, 60, 65, 76, 88, 109, 122, 125
kale, 112
Kansas City Barbecue, 69
kidney beans, 63
kimchi, 91
Lamb Kabobs with Tzatziki, 106
Lemon Chicken and Yam, 100
lemon juice, 110, 115, 118
lemon, 77, 100, 103
lentils, 108
lime juice, 32, 87, 93, 106, 108, 121
lime, 24, 36, 43, 79, 94, 121
Low-Country Shrimp and Grits, 80
Mango Coconut Sticky Rice, 121
mango, 50, 55, 121
marshmallows, 116
masa, 84
Massaman Chicken Curry, 87
Mayan Shredded Pork, 32
Mexican Green Rice, 10, 35, 39, 43, 44, 46, 55, 59, 66, 88, 108
Mexican Red Rice, 10, 27
Mini Apple Chimichangas, 115
mint, 106
Mongolian Beef, 96
Monterey Jack cheese, 16, 18, 36, 45, 49, 50, 52, 63, 64, 73, 77, 79, 81, 91, 94, 99, 100, 102, 107, 108, 109
mozzarella cheese, 112
Mushroom Fajitas, 60
mushroom, 53, 60, 94, 95
negro chile, 28
New Mexico Frito Pie, 84
New Orleans Red Beans and Rice, 63
nori, 93
okra, 64
Old World Posole, 39

orange juice, 27, 28, 32, 36, 39, 44
orange, 24, 43, 46, 55, 103
parsley, 74, 110
peanut butter, 61, 87
pear, 91
peas, 110
pepitas, 105
pepper jack cheese, 53, 63, 65
Picadillo Turkey, 102
pico de gallo, 24, 30, 32, 40, 103
pineapple juice, 27, 99
pineapple, 27, 44, 76, 77, 99
pinto beans, 29, 30, 60, 61, 65
poblano, 15, 56, 60, 125
Pork al Pastor, 27
pork, 27, 32, 39, 69, 73, 76
potato, 13, 15, 16, 19, 87, 012
queso fresco, 20, 30, 59, 80
Quick Refried Beans, 6
quinoa, 45, 52
radish, 39, 88
raisins, 102, 122
Ranch Breakfast, 19
ranch dressing, 66
Ranch Style Beans, 44, 84
Red Chile Adobo Beef, 28
Red Chile Mole, 35, 122
red curry paste, 87
Red Enchilada Sauce, 10, 83, 124
refried beans, 14, 15, 16, 27, 36, 53, 56, 79, 94, 103, 107, 109
Rib-eye Bahn Mi, 88
rice, 10, 27, 33, 39, 44, 55, 59, 63, 64, 74, 77, 79, 87, 88, 91, 93, 94, 95, 96, 99, 108, 110, 121
Roasted Beets and Goat Cheese, 49
S'Mores Mini Chimichangas, 116
salmon, 46
salsa, 13, 24, 30, 32, 40, 44, 70, 79
scallops, 59, 74

Seafood Paella, 110
Shaoxing wine, 96
shrimp, 43, 55, 59, 64, 74, 77, 79, 80, 110
Slow-Cooker Machaca Beef, 40
Smoky Caramelized Butternut Squash, 52
snow peas, 95
Southern Fried Chicken, 65
Southwest Surf and Turf, 79
Southwest Tofu, 61
soy sauce, 91, 93, 95, 96, 99
spiced rum, 118
Spicy Crispy Shrimp with Mango, 55
Spicy Grilled Salmon with Citrus, 46
spinach, 53
stuffing, 81
Sushi, 93
sweet potato, 105
Tequila Lime Shrimp, 43
Tequila Sunrise Chicken and Peppers, 36
tequila, 36, 43
Thanksgiving Bounty, 81
tofu, 61
Tomatillo Cream Sauce, 59, 124
tomatillo, 29, 124, 125
tomato, 15, 20, 29, 33, 61, 64, 70, 74, 84, 105, 106, 122
Tortilla Preparation, 7
Traditional Rolled Burritos, 4
Triple Mushroom and Spinach, 53
turkey, 81, 102
Twice-Barbecued Chicken, 50
vanilla ice cream, 118
Veggie Mulligatawny, 108
walnut, 49, 116
water chestnuts, 95
West Texas Beef Barbacoa, 70
yam, 100
yogurt, 106, 107

Donna Kelly, a dedicated food fanatic and recipe developer, is the author of several bestselling cookbooks including *Quesadillas, French Toast, Virgin Vegan Everyday Recipes, 200 Appetizers, 101 Things to do with a Tortilla,* and *101 Things to do with Tofu.* She currently lives in Provo, Utah.

Sandra Hoopes is a culinary school graduate with an added pastry certificate and is the coauthor of *200 Appetizers.* She is currently the Food Editor for the Puma Press in Phoenix, Arizona.

METRIC CONVERSION CHART

Volume Measurements		Weight Measurements		Temperature Conversion	
U.S.	**Metric**	**U.S.**	**Metric**	**Fahrenheit**	**Celsius**
1 teaspoon	5 ml	$^1/_2$ ounce	15 g	250	120
1 tablespoon	15 ml	1 ounce	30 g	300	150
$^1/_4$ cup	60 ml	3 ounces	90 g	325	160
$^1/_3$ cup	75 ml	4 ounces	115 g	350	180
$^1/_2$ cup	125 ml	8 ounces	225 g	375	190
$^2/_3$ cup	150 ml	12 ounces	350 g	400	200
$^3/_4$ cup	175 ml	1 pound	450 g	425	220
1 cup	250 ml	$2^1/_4$ pounds	1 kg	450	230